Australian
Country
Houses

Australian
Country
Houses

Homesteads, Farmsteads and Rural Retreats

Clive Lucas
Ray Joyce, photography

compiled by Elaine Rushbrooke

Lansdowne Press
Sydney   Auckland   London

Photographer's note

Without the wonderful co-operation of the owners of all the houses featured in this book, their hospitality and their consent to photograph, this project would have indeed been difficult. Their understanding of my requests to take photographs at odd hours played an important part in producing this record. To those who gave me shelter and sustenance I am truly thankful. Credit and thanks must also go to Elaine Rushbrooke, an unsung 'author' of this project. It was Elaine's concept and it is her sensitive design that presents this book. Finally, my sincerest gratitude goes to Anne Wilson and Lansdowne Press who have supported this project wholeheartedly from the beginning.

Ray Joyce

A Kevin Weldon Production
Published by Lansdowne Press
a division of Weldons Pty Limited
372 Eastern Valley Way, Willoughby NSW 2068 Australia
First published 1987

© Photographs and design Weldons Pty Limited 1987
© Text Clive Lucas 1987

Produced in Australia by the Publisher
Typeset in Australia by Savage Type Pty Ltd, Brisbane
Printed in Singapore by Kyodo Printing Co. Pte Ltd
Designed by E. L. Rushbrooke

National Library of Australia Cataloguing-in-Publication Data

Lucas, Clive.
Australian country houses.

Bibliography
Includes index.
ISBN 0 7018 1974 X.

1. Country homes — Australia — History — 19th
century. 2. Architecture, Domestic — Australia —
History — 19th century. 3. Interior decoration —
Australia — History — 19th century. I. Joyce, Ray,
1947– . II. Title.
Rushbrooke, Elaine III. Title

728.3'7'0994

Contents

Acknowledgements

6

Preface

7

Late Georgian

8

Early Victorian

40

Mid Victorian

72

Late Victorian

88

Bibliography

122

Glossary

123

Index

126

Acknowledgements

A book like this is in part the result of visiting country houses. Looking at old buildings has been a passion with me as long as I can remember, undoubtedly nourished by my family's pioneering history on the Hawkesbury and in south-western Queensland. The passion for architecture may well result from the fact that my great-great-grandfather first came to New South Wales in 1814 on the same ship that brought our first architect, Francis Greenway, to Australia. I visited my first homestead when I was a schoolboy, and pursuing my childhood ambition to become an architect encouraged me to continue to visit country houses whenever I could, both here and abroad.

Seeing is not all that is necessary to write a book such as this; one also needs historical information. This has been gleaned from many sources, not least of which is the ever-growing library of books on Australia's 200-year architectural and historical story. The published works that have been consulted are listed later in the bibliography.

As a conservation architect I have been privileged to work on the restoration of numerous country houses – Malahide, Clarendon, Rosedale and Bookanan among them – and they have been included in this book.

Thus I owe a debt to many people: my clients, those who have taken me to houses, those who have shared their considerable knowledge with me, but above all the owners of the houses who have allowed me to visit and share their private worlds. I thank them for their hospitality and for answering the enquiring letters I have written to them in relation to this book.

To all those who have helped me I am most grateful, but in particular Roderick Agar, Mr and Mrs Alastair Angas, James Archer, Thomas Archer, Mr and Mrs John Bagot, Mr and Mrs Charles Bagot, Miss Georgina Bassingthwaighte, D. D. Beaumont, T. J. Beaumont, Miss Pamela Bell, Dr James Broadbent, Dr B. G. Burbury, Mr and Mrs N. D. Burbury, Mrs Hugh Cameron, Mr and Mrs Alan Cameron, Thomas Lindesay Clark, Alistair Cox, Graham Crowley, Mrs. B. Q. Deane, Mr and Mrs Alexander Dennis, Mr and Mrs S. Doble, Mrs G. S. Douglas, Lady Downer, Mrs J. Dunne, Mr and Mrs Timothy Emanuel, Mr and Mrs Lyster Foster, Mrs Arthur Fox, Mr and Mrs Robert Gatenby, Miss Susan Gibson, Mr and Mrs Andrew Gibson, Mr and Mrs J. G. Gosse, Mrs Richard Green, Mr and Mrs William Hawke, Mrs James Hawker, Mrs J. Hodgson, P. C. James, Mrs P. D. Johnson, Mrs Brian Johnstone, Mrs S. Jones, Dr Miles Lewis, Nigel Lewis, Fergus McArthur, D. C. McConnel, Mr and Mrs D. MacDonald, Mr and Mrs R. K. McFarlane, Mrs Arthur MacKinnon, Mr and Mrs Donald MacKinnon, Mr and Mrs James Mac Smith, Edward Manifold, Mrs Irwin Maple-Brown, James Maple-Brown, Marbury School, Mr and Mrs Malcolm Melrose, Mr and Mrs M. D. Mills, John Morris, Mr and Mrs A. E. P. Mort, Mr and Mrs James Mort, The National Trust of Australia, Mrs George Nicholas, Andrew Nicolson, Mrs Athol Nicolson, The Hon. Mrs Patrick O'Neill, Mr and Mrs John O'Shanesy, Mrs J. M. Oxley, Miss Heather Philp, Mrs Charles Ransom, D. A. Rea, Mr and Mrs R. B. Ritchie, Mrs and Mrs Richard Royds, Geoffrey Stilwell, Miss Rosemary Stilwell, The Hon. Rose Talbot, the Misses J. and L. Tourle, Mr and Mrs Thomas Tourle, Bruce Wall, Mrs A. E. Walmsley, Mr and Mrs Ronald Watson, Peter Watts, Mrs C. G. Wilson and W. J. Yates.

Finally I must thank my partner Ian Stapleton for his patience and advice and my secretary Elisabeth Stewart who typed the almost indecipherable handwritten manuscript as well as all the letters sent to people. But an undertaking like this cannot be done without the support of one's family. To my wife Sarah and my children Adelaide, Georgina and William I owe a special thank you.

Clive Lucas

Preface

In 1788, when Europeans first built in this country, British architecture was in what has become known as its neo-classical period, a period when architects and gentlemen created buildings inspired by past periods of architectural greatness. Greek, Roman, Egyptian, Gothic, Etruscan, even Chinese architecture formed a basis for building design. Indeed ever since the middle of the eighteenth century when gentlemen had travelled to faraway places such as Egypt and China, new concepts had influenced architectural thought. It was in this atmosphere that Australian architecture was born, although preoccupation with style was hardly something to concern the struggling colonists until at least the teens of the nineteenth century, by which time some order and means of survival had been established.

The story of the Australian house is really that of the country house, because although houses have been built in towns which can be described as urban – being terraced and attached in some way – the vast majority are detached, and many houses of consequence built in inner districts of cities are little different from what is to be found in the country. The first house of consequence to be built was for the Governor at Sydney in 1788. It was in essence a country house, of the farmhouse or small rectory type, a design that could be described as vernacular or provincial Georgian. It is very like Greenhouse, which is a contemporary farmhouse at Tullowmagimma in Co. Carlow, Ireland.

A country house book is by nature a book on consequential houses. It is a book about the houses built by men of consequence in locations that were considered of importance. They are houses that fulfil more than the basic needs of their owners, and in the parlance of the nineteenth century they are gentlemen's houses, houses of architectural pretension and of style. Many of the designs had their source in the bourgeoning production of architectural pattern books which commenced publication in the late eighteenth century and were purchased by architects and gentlemen alike. From the mid nineteenth century there were the building magazines as well.

To call them country houses in the English sense is perhaps wrong, in that their size rarely approached even that of a small manor house. Also, all of them are not principal residences on landed estates. In other words, not all were homesteads. Some were country retreats for merchants or professional men who made their livelihood in the town or city. Many would have been described as villa residences by both their architects and their proprietors.

The term 'country house' has been used so that we abandon the idea that only country houses that are homesteads exist in Australia. The book attempts to exemplify houses of architectural pretentiousness and character that were built outside the towns and cities of Australia during the nineteenth century.

C.L.L.
December 1986

Late Georgian

This book concerns itself with what survives, and it is hoped that by illustrating such houses it will encourage people to help them continue to survive as examples of architecture worth keeping. This, after all, is the reason they have been included in the book.

Although our story starts in 1788 it is hard to find an intact example before about 1820 in the territories where Europeans built in New South Wales and Tasmania. A significant place to start is at **Richmond Hill**, built *c.*1823 in Tasmania, a house that is vernacular Georgian, just like the first Government House at Sydney in 1788. There is no verandah, and its perfectly balanced facade – stuccoed single-storey five-bay, broken into three by strong pilasters and centred on a large fanlit Georgian doorway – makes one think of Ireland, of the sort of houses found in suburbs of Dublin and illustrated in Maurice Craig's *Classic Irish Houses of the Middle Size.* Unlike its Irish cousins, Richmond Hill is not raised on a semi-basement of service rooms, and its proprietor does not seem to have come from or been to Ireland. Maybe it is the builder who had the Irish experience.

Top *Richmond Hill has a quality one associates with Irish Georgian architecture. The large central fanlit front door in fact relates many Australian colonial houses more closely to Irish architecture than to anything English.*

Left *The utilitarian nature of stables often makes them less formal than houses, with a timeless vernacular quality. Materials too are usually more basic. Here the walls are of random rubble which has been once limewashed.*

Above *The front walls of the house are harled and the front door, with its fanlight and surrounding symmetrical window panes, is typical of what most Australians expect an early colonial front door to look like.*

A more sophisticated house, in Tasmania, is **Lake House**. This is a house that ornaments its landscape and can be seen for miles around. There is a complete basement for the offices, with an area behind so that the house is clear all round, the *beau idéal* of early nineteenth century architects. An area is the space below ground level, between the main wall and a retaining wall, as a precaution against dampness and to provide light and air to the basement. The main three-bayed two-storey block is flanked by single-storey wings. Each bay of the parapeted stuccoed walls is accentuated by being recessed and separated by pilaster piers and the whole centred on a timber porch of the pure Greek Doric order. Of the many styles of neo-classicism, Greek was the

most popular, and in the years after Napoleon's final defeat at Waterloo it was used for almost all articles of design. Lake House is a true villa design, possibly taken from an architect's pattern book or else commissioned by an architect and brought out by the London merchant who settled in Tasmania and built the house *c.*1830.

Inside has a cruciform hall with bold arches at the crossing. Originally the walls were painted in imitation of slabs of granite. At the back a geometrical stair rises to the chamber floor above and descends to the offices in the basement. The transverse hall leads to the two wings, which are handsome single rooms with high ceilings and tall embrasured windows. The joinery is all cedar, and the principal chimneypieces are, like the porch, in the Greek Doric order. The room to left of the front door was Robert Corney's library and has elegant glazed and fitted bookcases balancing the chimneybreast.

Early nineteenth century gentlemen in Australia lived in either verandahed cottages or

The Greek revival was the most popular style of the late Georgian period, being used in all facets of design. At Lake House the pure Greek Doric order is used for the beautiful timber porch.

The same attention to detail shown in the porch is carried inside. The library has fitted bookcases balancing its Grecian chimneypiece. The wood is cedar from the east coast of New South Wales which strongly resembles mahogany, the then fashionable timber for quality furniture in England.

Above right *The plan of the main block of the house is set out around a cruciform of corridors. At the back is the principal stair, geometric in form, which as well as going up goes down to the basement kitchen and service rooms. Originally the walls were finished in imitation of granite. In the front hall are rails originally for hat and coat hooks.*

Right *Lake House is a classical villa, its walls beautifully articulated in the chaste Grecian mode. Balancing the main block are the principal reception rooms and under the centre are its basement offices. The house could be seen all round unencumbered by service wings.*

Left *The verandahed bungalow was a common form for a late Georgian house in Australia. Clairville, with its verandah under the main roof, suggests its builder had experience of British colonial architecture in India, West Indies or South Africa.*

Below *Chair rails were almost universally used in Georgian architecture. They became unfashionable after c.1830 and many have since been removed. In this room the rail or surbase survives together with the even rarer contemporary French panoramic wallpaper depicting Napoleon's arrival in Egypt.*

Front doors are often the focus for the joiner's craftsmanship. At Clairville chinoiserie, one of the more exotic aspects of British neo-classicism, has been used for the glazing patterns in the fanlight and sidelights.

At the entrance to the drive to the house is a toy-like formal neo-classical gate lodge, its rendered walls nicely articulated, suggesting at least that a pattern book was used as source for its design.

villas. Although the verandahed form we will see at Malahide could have been influenced by houses on the south coast of England, the form of a house like **Clairville** would certainly seem to suggest a more exotic influence. Its builder, John Sinclair, may have been to India or one of the other British colonies where men built bungalows. Here the verandah is under the main roof, all supported by a tall colonnade. The present colonnade has almost certainly lost some of the detail of the original design; it was probably more consciously in one style or other.

The plan form here is a corridor running across the house with the main door at the side, leaving the front for the tall main rooms with french doors to open on to the verandah. Behind the corridor the house is a storey and a half high, with attics under the roof.

Inside the joinery is cedar with a handsome front door and chimneypieces. The centre room on the principal front retains the rare feature of an intact chair rail with a French panoramic wallpaper above as witness to the refined taste of some colonial gentlemen. The paper is thought to depict the arrival of Napoleon in Egypt in 1798.

At the entrance to the drive is a decorative gate lodge. A pavilion, square on plan, it has elaborately panelled walls and a dominant central chimney.

The *beau idéal* of a house in the round, a pretty pavilion, taxed the minds of many a colonial gentleman builder. One such gentleman was James Gordon. Gordon's father was a steward to the Duke of Northumberland, and his connexions had given him high office in Tasmania: naval officer at Hobart and later magistrate at Richmond. However, his behaviour was found wanting, particularly with regard to the consumption of alcohol, and he was dismissed from office in 1835. Despite this cloud he did manage to erect **Forcett House**. Forcett is a pavilion of the loveliest brick, a square on plan, capped with a glazed lantern for viewing the surrounding estuaries of the Derwent River. The service wing is separate to the side but linked to the house by garden walls to form a service court. The main block has three principal elevations. The brick walls are subtly broken into bays centred on windows of the loveliest design. The main door is balanced on one side by a dummy window painted in *trompe-l'oeil*, and the return elevation with the adjoining principal rooms was built with venetian windows set low in the wall so that the beautiful views from the rooms would be unimpaired. The third front is centred on a windowed door to keep the rhythm intact.

Like a number of the houses discussed in this chapter, Forcett hides the fact that it is on more than one level at the back; and in the central hall, reached from an outer hall, a phalanx of doors conceals the staircase, cupboards and access to the rear of the house. Forcett is a complex design and therefore must have had an architect, but no one is known or even suggested. It is certainly unique in Australia.

Left *Forcett House is sited on one of the estuaries of the River Derwent and its central roof lantern makes it possible to take in distant views of these idyllic waterways.*

Below *Flemish bonded brickwork of exceptional quality and chaste stone detailing around the beautifully refined joinery of the venetian window in the principal front of the house epitomise the best of Georgian architecture.*

Centre *The main block of the house has three fronts free to take in views of the countryside. On the left is the entrance front and facing are the venetian windows which light the interconnecting principal rooms.*

Above *Like many colonial houses there is often an outer and inner hall connected by a fanlit door. The central hall is dominated by doorways which provide access to the inner reaches of the house.*

Forcett conceals from the front that it has attics. The stair from the central hall provides access to these rooms and to the viewing lantern above.

Over *One often thinks of Tasmania as green and English, but many parts are quite Australian. Forcett is a late Georgian house set down in pastoral landscape.*

Perhaps the most sophisticated of all Greek revival facades in Australia is that at Panshanger. It suggests the hand of a trained architect, although none is known. It was originally a storey and a half high but the attics were removed in 1920.

The elegant stone front built in 1831–34 is in fact an addition to an earlier brick house which forms one side of a courtyard at the back of the house.

More grand, more scholarly, more spectacular is the main block of **Panshanger** in northern Tasmania, built by Joseph Archer who conceived his estate on a grand scale with many substantial and decorative outbuildings, an elaborate pleasure garden, rides and park. Panshanger has a beautiful facade at the centre of this whole ensemble overlooking the pleasure garden. The house here suggests a growth of ideas and incorporates the earlier house at the back. The facade was perhaps obtained to tie the whole together, and it and the main block were the culmination of Archer's ambitions.

Inside the house is quite conventional: the paved hall balanced by the principal rooms which open on to the terrace; and behind, a cross hall leading to the rooms at the end. At the rear are the service wings linked by walls to the stables and numerous outbuildings. What the house lacks in concept it makes up for in detail, including the beautiful statuary marble Greek revival chimneypiece with caryatids in the drawing room, the fine plasterwork in the hall and principal rooms, the beautiful gateway that leads to the service yard behind, and of course the crisply detailed Grecian facade which almost suggests the individual hand of an English architect such as Sir John Soane (1753–1837). Panshanger, unlike the other scholarly villas which were built and finished, is the culmination of a gentleman's achievement over many years and exemplifies his growth in wealth and sophistication.

In England the early nineteenth century was the 'age of mahogany'. In Australia the local cedar was a wonderful substitute. It was used lavishly not only for furniture, but for all the joinery of a house. Such detail would not be found in houses in England. There it would be plaster or carried out in deal and painted.

Above left *The first glimpse of the house is at the end of a long dark avenue. The beautifully articulated facade looks out over a broad sward of lawn centred on a decorative stone fountain.*

Left *As is usual in many late Georgian houses, the front hall is stone flagged. A cross hall runs across the back of the principal rooms. The joinery is of native cedar with typical six-panelled doors. High skirtings make it up to date in contrast with the low skirting board and chair rail of conservative late Georgian designs.*

The central tablet of the drawing room chimneypiece depicts the selling of cupids, a theme popular with neo-classical artists. The only other known chimneypiece of this kind is at nearby Woolmers, the home of Joseph Archer's brother.

The elaborate Greek revival style statuary marble chimneypiece in the drawing room, together with its fitted register grate, were imported from England for the house by Joseph Archer.

Malahide, in the Fingal valley, Tasmania, is another type of country house built by a gentleman: an ornamented farmstead, or *ferme ornée*. Malahide was built in 1834 for the Hon. William Talbot, scion of the ancient Anglo-Irish family of Talbot. The youngest son, he had come to seek his fortune in the wilderness. The decorative farmhouse he built is part of a conceived total complex.

Central to the concept was a quadrangle entered by a central gateway and around which were ranged not only the stables, the storehouses, the barn and coach-houses, but also the farmhouse and its offices. The gateway is balanced by the house on the left and by the kitchen and stables on the right. At the back facing each other across the quadrangle were the barn and the wool-store. Unfortunately the full intention of William Talbot's scheme was not realised, and the concept has been marred by later additions at the back.

The house at Malahide has an attractive light Regency verandah to distinguish it from the rest of the single-pile farm buildings. Seven bays along with a central door it is a storey and a half high. The house is sashed with inward-opening casements, and at the end under the verandah the windows have ogee-headed arches. Inside, the rooms on either side of the centre hall with its pretty geometrical stair were entered one from another. The doors and windows have plastered reveals, which befit the idea of a farmhouse. Typical of Tasmania, the window sashes are painted but the doors are polished.

Left *The light concave-roofed verandah is similar to those of Regency houses in the south of England. Ogee-headed windows are probably in deference to similar windows in Malahide Castle, William Talbot's ancestral home near Dublin.*

Above *The main entrance to the farmstead at Malahide is between the two balanced pavilions. That on the left contains the house, its front door focused by two pinus trees on the pyramidal St Patrick's Peak to the east of the house.*

The farmstead seen across the Break o'Day River. Half the completed complex is visible and in the foreground are the cottages for the men.

Top *From within the courtyard looking towards the original kitchen in the middle with the stables and coach-house to the left. The brick service wing added in the 1850s destroyed William Talbot's concept.*

Above right *The front hall is well detailed with elegant plasterwork and a geometric stair leading to the bedrooms in the half-storey above.*

Right *The dining room attained its present form in 1974; before 1964 it was two rooms in the original house. To the left of the door is a portrait of Samuel Talbot who succeeded his uncle William Talbot at Malahide in 1845.*

Opposite page, below *The windows are inward-opening casements and the sidelights have margin bars. Before 1964 the front wall of the house was more typically plastered in imitation of ashlar.*

Cambria, built in 1836, appears as a balanced single-storeyed bungalow with a front verandah. The house looks out over a formal garden, with box hedging and balancing bunya pines to the Meredith River and the sea.

The balanced back reveals the true nature of the house. It is built into a bank with a mezzanine across the back and attics under the roof. This front overlooks the old orchard and kitchen garden.

A house that is more obviously Australian, at least on its main front, is **Cambria** on the east coast of Tasmania. It is a bungalow with unusual french doors in panelled reveals, opening on to a deep diagonally flagged verandah which looks out over a geometrically designed garden to the Meredith River and Great Oyster Bay. The house is more intricate than is immediately apparent. The land falls away steeply at the back, and the rear facade is vernacular Georgian, two-storeyed with attics formed by mezzanines with the main floor of the house. The walls are harled or roughcast, and the elaborate dormers have glazed cheeks. Here the kitchen and offices were in the basement. It is a more complex example of the many colonial houses which on their main elevation conceal the fact that they have attic storeys.

It is really an atypical house. The entrance through french doors is off-centre of its four-bayed elevation, and inside the principal room of interest the front hall has balanced fanlit doors hiding the stairs, one up, one down. What inspired such a design is unclear. It could have been its proprietor's time in the navy which took him to such places as the West Indies. George Meredith who built it was known as 'King of Great Swanport' and was certainly an educated man from a professional family with origins in Devon and Wales. The house is well fitted with marble chimneypieces and was well furnished with imported furniture, amongst which was a grand pianoforte by Broadwood. It was built certainly to be comfortable and to create an impression as the principal house in the district. It was known as the 'Government House of the East Coast'.

In Britain in the 1820s a new influence affected English architecture. The Renaissance architecture of Italy was rediscovered and popularised chiefly by the young architect Charles Barry (1795–1860). In the same way as young architects in the eighteenth century had travelled afar – Robert Adam to Dalmatia, and William Chambers to China – so Barry had travelled the Mediterranean, especially visiting Rome and Florence, making sketches and taking notes. His Travellers' Club of 1829 in London's Pall Mall was his first building to show how the Italian *palazzo* could sensibly be adapted to a modern English building.

After this time, Italianate with Gothic was increasingly to transplant Greek as the principal style of modern English secular buildings and be popularised by such writings as J. C. Loudon's *Encyclopaedia of Cottage, Farm and Villa Architecture*, first published in 1833. This book became the bible for anyone wanting to build in England or the colonies, and most gentlemen's libraries contained a copy. It was reprinted in a number of editions until the 1860s, and Italianate was to become the most sensible and popular style of the early Victorian period. A number of Australian examples will be discussed in the next chapter.

It is often said that Australia lagged behind, that its buildings were old-fashioned and that Georgian architecture flourished here long after it had died in England. But this is no more true here than any provincial place, and New South Wales and Tasmania must be seen as no less provincial than, say, Scotland or Ireland. Certainly, once you had avant-garde publications like Loudon's book, gentlemen could be up to date anywhere.

The unusual front hall is entered by french doors to the right of the centre of the main elevation. Fanlit doors conceal the stairs, one leading up to the mezzanine, one going down to the kitchens.

Left *The verandah is unusually wide for a Tasmanian house. Unlike most colonial houses the main entrance door is neither central nor obvious. In many respects Cambria is rather like many Anglo-Indian colonial bungalows.*

Bicton is more Italianate in character than almost any other house of the 1830s. The Italian style was to supplant Greek revival as the most popular style of the early Victorian period.

The joinery is pine with only elements like paterae and consoles in cedar. The woodwork is now stripped and in the principal rooms there are fitted bookcases. Surviving in the dining room is cedar furniture of the early Victorian period.

Behind the house, across a large open yard, are the extensive stables and coach-houses built in the vernacular manner of the late Georgian period.

An example of this is **Bicton**, in Tasmania, which although apparently a conservative design has, by 1837 when it was built, details that relate directly to the Italianate style. The facade in brick and stone is at once more Italianate, and the treatment of the front doorcase with console brackets relates directly to Italianate models. Similarly, inside, the details of the four-panelled pine doors (as distinct from the more typical six-panelled doors of this period) are Italianate in feeling, as are the principal chimneypieces. Although a country house, Bicton with its blank side walls could well have been built in a town beside similar residences. This might also suggest that the Yorkshireman Andrew Gatenby, who had it built for one of his sons, obtained the design from some published source. The plan of the house is of a type found often in colonial Australia, the front hall screened from the staircase hall by large double doors,

with minor cross halls creating pantries and smaller rooms behind the large principal rooms balanced in the front. The fireplaces are at the sides balanced by fitted cupboards; and the double-hung windows are set in generous embrasures with shutter boxes.

Inside the stables, the utilitarian nature of the exterior late Georgian vernacular style gives way to horse stalls of the most delightful elaboration.

Wickford has the character of an Irish country house of the late Georgian period and supports the theory that much of the character of our colonial architecture derives from provincial Irish Georgian architecture.

A less up to date design but a contemporary house is **Wickford** built in 1838 by Henry Clayton, whose son William (1823–77) became an architect and later went to New Zealand where he was appointed Colonial Architect. There is a suggestion that William may have designed Wickford as a boy before he went to England to be educated. This house is at once Georgian, like a two-storeyed Richmond Hill. Built of plain brick probably first unpainted, the five-bay elevation is centred on a large semi-circular fanlit door with engaged columns which stylistically belong to the Greek revival. This door is very Irish and is reminiscent of a doorway in a Dublin square. The house is designed in the round, with windows at the side, and it sits on a terrace running around three sides. The service buildings are set back and form a large quadrangle at the rear.

Inside, the hall runs through the house with only an archway to break it, and there is a geometrical stair climbing the back wall below an elegant window. Like other examples this house conceals the fact that it has an attic storey, and the stair rises through two floors. The joinery is cedar. The door and window cases with paterae (flat circular ornamentation in the form of a dish at the junction of the architraves) below a light entablature are strongly Georgian in character.

Far left *Elegant cedar doorcases reflect the rather old-fashioned late Georgian character of the house and one suspects the house could once have had chair rails.*

Left *The beautifully executed Greek-style front door is reminiscent of Dublin with a wonderful semi-circular fanlight. The four-panelled door contrasts to the six-panelled doors in the interior of the house.*

Wickford, built in 1838, exemplifies the late Georgian style. Its typical colonial front hall is broken by an archway. On the archway is the hook for the original hall lamp. A geometrical staircase climbs the back wall, overlooked by an elegantly designed window. The house may have been designed by a young William Clayton.

More spectacular and up to date is the house at **Clarendon** built in 1838 by James Cox, whose family had settled in New South Wales in 1800. The ambitions of Cox were similar to those of Joseph Archer at Panshanger, and the house is at the centre of a large pastoral establishment. Clarendon takes in the countryside about it and is approached up a broad hedged avenue focused on a barn. The house sits in its own pleasure garden to the right, laid out in the fashionable gardenesque manner. From the encircling carriage road the main front is first seen between hedgerows across the garden.

Clarendon is triumphantly neo-classical, and its influence would seem to be more French than Italian Renaissance. It is a house to be seen all round, raised on a high rusticated semi-basement of offices, with an encircling area walk. From the terrace, which breaks forward of its three central bays, rises a giant portico of Ionic columns. This order is then carried around the elevations with pilasters marking each bay. It is five bays by three, and a slight breakfront breaks the side elevations, which are blind except for the centre bay. The other principal elevation, which is centred on a fanlit doorway reached by stairs, looks out to the South Esk River across the walled flower garden and across the farmyard flanked by balancing ranges of vernacular barns and stables. The roof of the house is not meant to be seen, and the walls are crowned by an entablature of somewhat naive design broken by elaborate neo-classical chimneystacks which suggest the French Empire style. At one side are the outhouses hidden by garden walls which flank the kitchen garden. In the pleasure garden below the house is a picturesque privy in the Gothic style.

Inside the plan is unusual, almost early eighteenth century in concept, like the houses of the English architect Sir John Vanbrugh. The main front hall runs through the centre of the house, with fanlit entrance doors, at each end and the side walls broken by piers to form five bays each with a doorway. At the centre, cross halls lead off but these are hidden by tall fanlit doors. In the right-hand hall is the principal staircase, a geometrical stair of Tasmanian blackwood, which descends into the basement as well as rising to the chamber floor above. This hall is balanced by a hall containing secondary service staircases, which also go down to the basement offices.

There are six rooms on the main floor: large double rooms at the front, and pairs of single rooms at the back. The double rooms are the drawing room and dining room which have pairs of tall windows looking out into the pleasure garden. These rooms – like all those leading into the main hall – have two doorways. The large window sashes, while double-hung, present themselves as casements in that popular early-Victorian way. With the exception of the principal stair, all the joinery is pine, doors are four-panelled, chimneypieces are marble, and the plasterwork in the principal rooms is enriched by popular papier mâché decoration. Scale is noble at Clarendon.

Neo-classicism reached its high point with the construction of Clarendon in 1838. Its design relates to French rather than English neo-classicism. Comparisons with contemporary plantation houses in Louisiana are obvious.

Clarendon has a magnificence of scale unequalled elsewhere. The main front looks out over a generous carriage sweep to a garden laid out on fashionable gardenesque principles.

The house is raised on a high semi-basement with an encircling area walk. In the basement are the kitchens and domestic offices.

In contrast to the classical nature of the house the double privy in the garden is in the picturesque Gothic style.

Top *The carriage road skirts the extensive pleasure garden in front of the house and the main north front is first seen theatrically across a lawn defined by hawthorn hedges. Elms flank the facade.*

The south front of the house looks out to the river across a broad yard flanked by balancing stables and coach-houses. These buildings retain the English iron tiles that originally roofed the house.

Above left *The cross halls contain the staircases. The back servants' stair hall provides access to the service yard at the side of the house as well as down to the kitchens and up to the bedrooms.*

Left *The joinery throughout the house is pine and painted and, typical of the neo-classical house, the skirtings are high, here almost 600 millimetres. In the principal rooms the ceiling plasterwork is enriched with papier mâché. The elaborate marble chimneypiece in the drawing room is white; in the balancing dining room it is black.*

Durham Hall is by contrast a more typical country house of the late 1830s in New South Wales. George Hill, who built this house, was an emancipist, a convict who had made good. He had a large house of the same name in Sydney, and this, his country house, was no more than a cottage on an outstation more occupied by the manager than the proprietor. Nevertheless it has all those refinements we have come to associate with colonial cottage architecture.

It is a quintessential cottage residence. The house is weatherboarded, five bays wide, with a central six-panelled door below a simple fanlight, flanked by twelve-paned windows. Across the front is a verandah with a plastered soffit trimmed with a pretty valance and supported by wooden pilaster columns. Before all this is that rarest of survivals, an intact colonial cottage garden, geometrically arranged with box hedges which are now wonderfully mature. Behind, linked by a covered way draped with ancient wistaria, is the attic-roofed kitchen block with its servants' rooms and offices. This typically is of a lesser material, split vertical slab, colour-washed in a lovely red ochre.

Durham Hall is a weatherboarded verandahed cottage. An archetypal house of the late 1830s, it looks out over its geometrically arranged cottage garden.

At the rear of the house, reached by a covered way, is the kitchen block. Above it are the servants' rooms reached by a simple stair.

Left The verandah has a timber valance and the tapered timber columns are in the form of pilasters enriched by an applied mock panel.

A nineteenth-century photograph of Durham Hall, built in the late 1830s by emancipist George Hill, shows the house with its split shingled roof and the garden not yet grown to maturity. Its colonial cottage garden is still intact.

The covered way which joins the kitchens to the house is enclosed by lattice and in the courtyard is a mature wistaria vine of huge proportions.

Left The kitchen wing typically is of more primitive vernacular construction. Built of split slab with simple ledged doors, it is colour washed a lovely red ochre. Shingles can be seen above the verandah plate.

The kitchen block from the rear of the complex. The skillion dormer provides light to the rooms under the roof. Beyond are the tall pinus trees which mark the entrance to the garden before the house.

About contemporary with Durham Hall is **Bookanan** built *c.*1839, in the hills beyond Bathurst, New South Wales. This too is a cottage residence, five bays wide and a storey and a half high. It is a single-pile house with a skillion at the back over its kitchen and offices. Under the skillion is also the simple staircase, lit by a dormer window.

Bookanan is distinguished by massive stone walls and diminutive scale. It is a vernacular version of Malahide. The first-floor windows are casement and shuttered, and the flagged verandah across the front has simple ladder-framed columns. Inside there is a square front hall. There is good-quality cedar joinery of Georgian character, and the two balancing principal rooms have windows with panelled reveal shutters. Unlike Durham Hall, Bookanan was built as his principal residence by settler John Glasson.

Bookanan was built by Cornish settler John Glasson. Much of its special character undoubtedly derives from established Cornish building practices.

Under the front verandah the ceiling is not lined and the terrace is paved with random-coursed stone flags.

Below *The main elevation has sash windows under the verandah but upstairs there are inward-opening casements.*

The interior of Bookanan features elegant cedar joinery. The architraves are butted and mitred in the early way and above the front door is a fanlight. In contrast to the six-panelled front door, the internal doors are of four panels.

Top *The house is typical of many early colonial houses, a two-storeyed single pile front with a skillion at the back. Under the skillion at Bookanan are the kitchen and offices; the large kitchen chimney can be seen on the left.*

Left *Dalness was designed as a fashionable Italianate villa of the late 1830s. The main block was originally balanced at the back by two wings of which only the left-hand one now remains.*

An elegant Doric doorcase marks the entrance. The windows appear as casements but in fact are sash windows. The finish of the walls is unusual; one would expect the red brick to be stuccoed.

While old-fashioned vernacular traditions continued, certain settlers required something more fashionable. One such man was Allan MacKinnon, who in 1839 on his **Dalness** estate outside Launceston, built himself an Italianate villa which could well be found at the same time outside any town in England. The source of the design is not known, although the local architect Robert de Little (1808–76) may have had a hand in it. The style is Italianate, yet oddly constructed in red face-brick. It is raised on a semi-basement, two storeys high, three bays wide, broken by pilasters, with a recessed centre bay centred on an elaborate Doric doorcase. This breakback is picked up in the roof, which adds to the complexity of the design. The windows are double-hung, although (like those at nearby Clarendon) they present themselves as inward-opening casements.

Inside the plan is irregular and does not have the Georgian balance found in almost every house we have so far looked at. The hall runs through the house broken by an archway and widens at the back on the left to allow the geometrical stair to climb up the left-hand wall. The large double drawing room on the right is thus balanced by a single room on the left and a smaller room behind. This irregular planning hiding behind composed facades was to become more and more a characteristic of the Victorian villa residence. More interesting and livable plan forms, which gave rooms of different proportions and sizes, were in contrast to the sameness of rooms in earlier houses. Dalness has attractive cedar joinery in the Italian mode and, with the exception of the drawing room which has marble, fine timber chimneypieces.

Left *The interior of the house is more up to date than many contemporary houses. The hall, broken by an archway, broadens at one side at the back to take the geometric stair. The doors are four-panelled.*

The ground floor sitting room has a cedar chimneypiece which is in the same spirit as the elaborate Doric front doorcase. Attractive cedar joinery in the Italian style is a feature of Dalness.

The verandahed cottage is less common in Tasmania than in New South Wales, but one such house is **Coswell** on the east coast. The view includes its pretty cottage garden, overlooking Great Oyster Bay to the Freycinet Peninsula. Like all its cousins it is vernacular, Georgian in detail, with squat six-panelled doors and cosy rooms that befit a seaside cottage. It too has attics showing only at the back, which are reached by a narrow single-flight stair.

Coswell is a verandahed cottage by the sea. A half-glazed door serves as the entrance and there is a decorative valance to the verandah.

Inside Coswell, a simple steep stair leads to the attics which are lit by skylights in the back slope.

Above left *From the verandah with its simple stop chamfered posts the house looks out over a pretty cottage garden to Great Oyster Bay and beyond to the Freycinet Peninsula.*

The ground floor rooms are cosy and low with broad six-panelled cedar doors and fitted shelves for books and possessions.

Far left *Bush Greek is how one might best describe the Ionic colonnade added by Alexander Reid to his house at Ratho sometime before 1837. The primitive capitals are supported on simple tree trunks.*

Left *The front hall is more typical. Above the main door is an unusually low fanlight.*

Below *Tall cordylines mark the central entrance to the verandah where the colonnade breaks forward. Intriguing Gothic-style chimneys break the roof line.*

A verandahed house of quite different type is **Ratho** on the Clyde River in Tasmania, which was built by a Scottish settler, Alexander Reid. It is a stone house, built in several stages, with intriguing chimneys which are Gothic in character. Superimposed on it is an impressive colonnade of the most primitive 'bush Greek' detail. The shafts of the columns are mere tree trunks, and they carry primitively carved Ionic capitals below a wooden entablature. The colonnade, which is centred on the six-panelled front door of the house, is quite sophisticated in form; the columns are doubled at the corners and at the breakfront that marks the entrance. All this was achieved by 1837, as were the fanciful octagonal weatherboarded pigeon and fowl houses in the grounds. Mr Reid was obviously a settler interested in architectural style.

Greek revival was the pre-eminent style of English architecture from after Waterloo in 1815 until the early Victorian period of the 1840s. It was used for courthouses, churches, schools, indeed for every conceivable building. In Australia there are courthouses like Darlinghurst in Sydney, churches like St George's at Battery Point in Hobart and schools like the King's School at Parramatta. Large houses like Fernhill, in New South Wales, and Panshanger, in Tasmania, were all strongly Grecian in the composition of their elevation and in the detail of many of their principal features. However, these are large houses, and it is hard to find smaller houses that are as consistently Grecian. An exception

The colonnade, centred on the front door of Ratho, has a soffit of wide boards with cover battens and the terrace is paved with random-coursed stone flags.

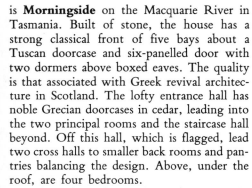

is **Morningside** on the Macquarie River in Tasmania. Built of stone, the house has a strong classical front of five bays about a Tuscan doorcase and six-panelled door with two dormers above boxed eaves. The quality is that associated with Greek revival architecture in Scotland. The lofty entrance hall has noble Grecian doorcases in cedar, leading into the two principal rooms and the staircase hall beyond. Off this hall, which is flagged, lead two cross halls to smaller back rooms and pantries balancing the design. Above, under the roof, are four bedrooms.

Other than the quality of the workmanship it is the style of the joinery at Morningside that is so arresting. There are fitted cupboards and elaborate shutter boxes to the large double-hung windows. In the principal rooms one chimneypiece is Doric, the other Ionic, while in one of the back rooms it is so highly mannerist as to suggest the individual hand of a Scottish architect such as Alexander ('Greek') Thomson (1817–75).

Morningside was built in 1839 for Waterloo veteran Claudius Thomson, a Scotsman. Hugh Kean, a builder/architect has been suggested as its architect. There are other houses in the district by him which are also distinguished by scholarly details but none quite as special as Morningside. Morningside has not been a principal residence for many years, and the detached kitchen and offices at the back are now derelict and the garden has disappeared.

Morningside is a house of a type associated with Scottish Greek revival architecture. The house sits above cellars that can be reached outside from the side or inside from the stair hall.

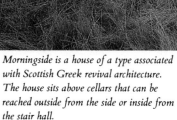

Above right The stair hall is separated from the front hall by a half-glazed door with an intriguing glazing pattern. In the front hall the doorways carry heavy Greek revival doorcases.

Left The highly mannerist chimneypiece in a back room has a composition normally associated with contemporary piered wardrobes.

Below In the original dining room (left) the chimneypiece is in the pure Greek Doric order. By contrast in the drawing room (centre) the chosen order is the Greek Ionic. The fourth chimneypiece on the ground floor (right) makes use of the Greek acroterion for its scholarly design.

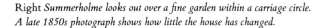

For the early 1840s, this doorway is old-fashioned. Its fanlight, margined sidelights and six-panelled door are typical early colonial features.

Right *Summerholme looks out over a fine garden within a carriage circle. A late 1850s photograph shows how little the house has changed.*

A contemporary house (although incorporating an earlier dwelling) which has continued to flourish with all its appurtenances is **Summerholme**, the country house of Henry Hopkins, a Hobart merchant, where we find all the details of the colonial country house. Before the house is a wonderful pleasure garden laid out in geometrical box hedging within the large carriage circle. To the left of the house is a wonderful greenhouse in front of the stables, with flagged walled yard between the house and its kitchen offices.

For the early 1840s Summerholme is old-fashioned, more Regency than early Victorian in character. A light verandah originally covered in oilcloth runs around three sides of the house, supported on turned timber posts.

The main front is of three bays, with casement doors balancing the main fanlit door, and above at first-floor level there are inward-opening casements. The walls are capped by parapets which hide the roof and its attic skylights. Inside, the main hall runs down the centre of the house, with the staircase at the back. Off the hall at the front are balancing rooms of Georgian character with large chimneypieces detailed with paterae. Surviving in the house are two wallpapers of the 1850s: in the front hall a baroque Great Exhibition paper in browns, and in the drawing room leading off it a grey paper simulating buttoned silk. With its surviving furnishings, gardens and outhouses, Summerholme exemplifies that quintessential colonial country establishment. When compared with photographs

taken in the 1850s, Summerholme in unchanged; only the garden has matured.

We have so far looked at houses that are in essence classical, detailed in ways that make them either continuing Georgian, or Grecian or Italianate. However, one of the great survivals in English architecture was Gothic, which in the eighteenth century started a revival as part of picturesque taste and became just as much a neo-classical style as Greek, Egyptian or Italian, reaching its peak in the mid nineteenth century. It was always thought of as somewhat frivolous when compared with the more masculine Greek and Italian styles, so in a land as harsh as Australia it is perhaps not surprising that at least in the early colonial period, it was not chosen for country houses. Nevertheless there are a few

Above left *This fine settle of late Georgian design is featured in the late 1850s photograph.*

Left *The hall wallpaper reflects the baroque taste of the early Victorian period.*

The wonderful early Victorian greenhouse is an important surviving element of the garden.

The dining room is lit by inward-opening casements and the early Victorian furniture sits on a red Turkey carpet.

Below *The front hall is broken by an arch with its geometric stair at the back; an early candle lamp hangs from the ceiling rose.*

The drawing room in the front of the house, which has casement doors on to the verandah, retains its early Victorian window cornices and wallpaper.

Right *Papier mâché drawing room side chairs in front of the paper purchased in 1852. The high skirting is a clue to the date of the front of the house.*

At the side of Henry Hopkins' retreat, Summerholme, between the house and the red brick stables, is a paved service yard with underground tank for drinking water.

exemplars, of which Kelvin Grove on the Ben Lomond River in Tasmania and Pomeroy on the Wollondilly River in New South Wales are prominent. To build such houses needed educated taste and a strong feeling for the picturesque. **Pomeroy** was built by Thomas Woore who had been a naval officer and had acquired skill as a surveyor. He drew well and obviously had a taste for artistic matters. Pomeroy is a Gothic villa with a deliberately perverse plan; its elevation is broken by tall gables of varying sizes, one of which forms a porch leading into the front hall from which rises the stair covered by a intriguing plaster ceiling of Gothic form.

While it is rare to find Gothic houses in the wilds, they were common enough as villas on the shores of Port Jackson, Sydney, or on the Derwent River, Hobart, which were no doubt considered more civilised environments in which to be frivolous. Nevertheless, even though they were not necessarily Gothic, extravagant architectural houses were built deep

Left *Picturesque Gothic is an unusual style for the Australian house in the country. Tall Tudor chimneys enliven the design.*

Below left *The simple Gothic porch at the front of Pomeroy constructed by Lieutenant Thomas Woore.*

Below centre *The front hall has a plastered tent form ceiling enriched by classical papier mâché decoration. The contrast of Gothic and classical was quite common at the time.*

Below *The ceiling detail is carried above the staircase which has cast-iron balusters also of classical design.*

Perhaps the most strikingly Georgian design of the colonial period is Killymoon in Tasmania, built in 1842 for Frederick von Stieglitz. The house, which is approached across river flats, sits proudly above a high terrace wall. Although its detail is Italianate, its concept is firmly fixed within the style of the eighteenth century.

in the country. One has only to think of Aberglasslyn in New South Wales and Killymoon in Tasmania to recall certain settlers' building ambitions. **Killymoon** is nothing like its castellated Irish namesake designed by John Nash in *c.*1803. It is, however, remarkably Irish in character. When the Duke of Wellington (1885–1972) (who as Lord Gerald Wellesley was a noted Georgian revival architect) visited the house in the 1960s he described it as strained in every proportion. And indeed it is. Its design is extraordinary.

Raised on a tall rusticated semi-basement, its tall facades of fine ashlar with bold string coursing are broken into bays by slight breakfronts; facing the sides are balancing three-sided bays; centred at the front is a three-sided bay with a light Doric portico which plants itself on the elevation in such a way as to suggest an individual architect of the type of Sir John Soane. There are parapets and bold chimneystacks of individual appearance. The main door leads into a broad hall running through the centre of the house, with an imperial stair at the back rising to the chamber floor and going down to the basement kitchen and other offices. Off the hall at the front are the two principal rooms with their bowed ends and their tripartite window arrangement and heavy plasterwork. Behind these are two rectangular rooms. The detail of the house is Italianate yet the concept is eighteenth century and original.

Before the house is a broad apron of gravel and a bollarded high retaining wall to separate it from the countryside. Balancing the facade at the sides beyond the principal rooms are brick garden walls with the decorative gateways shielding the kitchen garden on the left and the flower garden on the right. At the back the house looks out over its area to the large stable yard with an intriguing picturesque Gothic coach-house complete with turret clock and lantern dominating one end of the quadrangle. Killymoon was built in 1842 for an Irishman, Frederick von Stieglitz, and the builder is said to be the same man who built Clarendon several years before.

Left The house has a full basement for its extensive kitchen and office spaces with an area at the back and down the sides.

The intriguing coach-house with its picturesque Gothic windows stands at the end of the large stable yard behind the house.

Top *The plan form's preoccupation with shapes is reflected in the stair hall at Killymoon which runs through the centre of the house dominated by an imperial stair, a rare feature to find in a colonial house of the period. Coloured glass often appeared in fanlights to front doors after the 1840s.*

The dining room features heavy plasterwork and a black marble chimneypiece. It still contains some of its original furniture, dating from the mid nineteenth century. Upholstered armchairs and a couch are often found as part of the extensive furnishings of early Victorian dining rooms.

A house that is similar to Summerholme is **Streanshalh** in midland Tasmania. Here, however, the roof has generous overhanging eaves in the Regency way, and the roof has a bellcast. The windows of the three-bayed front are fitted with inward-opening casements, and under the verandah the french doors are without kickboards and their pretty glazing is taken down to the floor. Unlike the walls of most colonial houses which have a smoothly stuccoed imitation ashlar finish, here the walls are heavily rusticated under the verandah, and above the corners are strengthened by quoins which give the house its particular character. Entry is via a fanlit set of double doors into a hall, which runs the length of the house, with a dog-legged stair at the back. At the front the hall is balanced by the Georgian-proportioned dining and drawing rooms, which look out through french doors to the pretty garden before the house. Downstairs the joinery is typically 1840s, six-panelled doors with mitred architraves, but upstairs it is more elaborate, seemingly earlier and Georgian in character. There are paterae to the doorcases and chair rails to the walls. These are details that tended to disappear from colonial architecture after about 1830. Streanshalh was built over a number of years in the 1830s (it was still incomplete in 1842) by a Yorkshireman who had served under Nelson: Captain Francis Allison. He lies buried under a white marble obelisk on a small knoll in the valley below the house.

Many would say that the verandahed bungalow was the typical Australian house in the country, and this will be seen as correct as we continue our story. However, the verandah was not used universally, and many verandahs were not added until somewhat later. Sydney's first Government House had a verandah added in 1796, and Rouse Hill in N.S.W. (built in 1813) had one added in 1858, and so on. These houses were of the vernacular Georgian type, and if they had verandahs from the start they were treated like Malahide, much as they might have been if built on the south coast of England at the same time.

It is those houses where the verandah is integral to the design that have more exotic influences suggestive of India or the British colonies in the West Indies or Africa. Clairville is one house we have seen that suggests such experience, although its builder John Sinclair is not known to have been to such places. Maybe just a visit to Cape Town on the voyage out was enough, or maybe he obtained a design from some exotic sources. And anyway why build an Anglo-Indian bungalow in a temperate climate like Tasmania? Many did, Quamby and Mt Pleasant to name just a couple of houses.

A more understandable place to build a house of this type is Adelaide, where it gets quite hot in the summer. **Marybank** is such a house, and it was built by Captain Thomas Shepherd who had been in India in the army. This bungalow has its verandah integrated

The heavily rusticated walls are unusual. The verandah colonnade was rebuilt in the late Victorian period.

Top *Streanshalh took many years to build, which probably accounts for its old-fashioned appearance. The bellcast roof is a common feature of the late Georgian period.*

Right *The beautiful front door is in two leaves, the sidelights have margin bars and the panels of the door are elaborately fielded.*

Opposite page *The combination of fine colonial cedar furniture glimpsed through the equally fine margined french doors is a poignant reminder of the standard of colonial craftsmanship.*

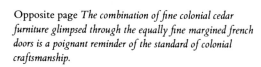

Marybank is an asymmetrical verandahed bungalow built by Captain Thomas Shepherd, an ex-Indian army officer. The front door was originally off-centre between the french doors. From the drawing room to the right there was a view across the side verandah to the Adelaide plain below.

with the design. The lesser pitch of the roof over the verandah gives the roof the broken back or bellcast that is such a feature of the rural Australian house. The roof, like that of almost every house we have seen, was originally shingled, but is now covered by the ubiquitous corrugated iron – which like the roof form itself is as Australian as thatch is to Norfolk or Wessex. At the edge the roof of Marybank is supported on heavy square posts, with the arrises removed to create deep stop chamfers, and at the verge of the roof is a box gutter treated as a simple entablature to the posts. The soffit of the verandah is plastered, as are the limestone walls of the house. Being in South Australia, the verandah is flagged not with sandstone but with slate from the quarries at Willunga.

Marybank is more complicated than most bungalows and has that perversity of plan often associated with more architectural villas. The five-bay elevation has the front door off-centre (it is now altered), with the drawing room running down the right-hand side and a pair of french doors giving a view across the verandah to the Adelaide plain below. To the left of the front hall was a small single-bay room and then two bays for the dining room. The two principal rooms have panelled reveals to their french doors, which are without kickboards and are fitted with shutters externally. There is good bold plasterwork on the ceilings and classical marble chimney-pieces. In the dining room there is a bellpull that survives, a silk cord with tassle, linked to

one of the eight spring bells in the scullery.

Here the service rooms are off to the left, leaving two main verandahed elevations to capture the main view. Sited on a terrace in the foothills behind Adelaide, Marybank has the quality of a site in Italy or Spain, with its groves of olives and mature garden.

In any discussion involving architecture there is the need to break it down into periods, if not into styles. We have opted for the first. In so doing we have tried to put under 'late Georgian' those buildings that stylistically fit best in this period. But, of course, there is a fine line separating periods, and many of the houses built in the 1840s could as well have been treated as early Victorian. For although there was a change in architectural attitudes in the early years of Queen Victoria's reign, that change did not happen at any exact time so there must of necessity be an overlap. One of the reasons for change was undoubtedly the writings of Loudon and especially his *Encyclopaedia of Cottage, Farm and Villa Architecture* first published in 1833. It was a great taste setter, as were the English building magazines of the time; the *Builder* started in 1843, the *Building News* in 1855, and so on. No longer did gentlemen need to build from memory or from some precious publication they had managed to acquire. There were now numerous publications to assist them as well as a growing profession of architects. Thus houses with more early Victorian pretensions are dealt with in the next chapter.

The two-panelled front door with its typical fanlight is now located at the side of the house.

Top *The french doors have margin bars but no kick panels and are fitted with louvred shutters against the sun.*

The stylish white marble chimneypiece in the dining room has later tiling and marble fender. The tassled servants' bellpull on the left is a rare survivor of early technology; linked by a wire it activated a spring bell in the scullery at the back of the house.

Opposite page, below *The long verandah across the front of the house is supported by heavy stop chamfered posts. The slate-paved verandah is typical of South Australia where sandstone is not common.*

The drawing room now combines two rooms of the original house. It features bold plasterwork on the ceiling and a classical marble chimneypiece. Marybank has a somewhat perverse plan for a bungalow, associated with villas of more architectural pretensions.

The dining room has robust plasterwork and panelled reveals to the french doors. The Jacobean-style fumed oak furniture dates to just after World War I when this style of furnishing was popular in Australia.

Early Victorian

Queen Victoria came to the throne in 1837, succeeding her uncle William IV and his consort Queen Adelaide. Such an event did not change architectural style overnight, but nevertheless there were several movements afoot which did mean that at about this time buildings appeared less wholeheartedly Georgian. The frivolity of the Regency years 1811–20 changed the simple innocence of Georgian architecture, and the influence of the revivals of Greek, Egyptian and Renaissance architecture gave a stylistic structure to the way buildings looked. This was further enriched by the picturesque idea of a villa and a building in the round.

Most houses now had at least two fronts; buildings were meant to be seen from the angle and not elevationally as most had been before when one front was considered pre-eminent. Then a large house might have had an entrance front and a garden front, each seen separately. In modern houses of the period these two fronts were at right angles to each other and the house was meant to be viewed at 45 degrees, and gardens and approaches were set out to highlight this. In striving for the picturesque, buildings also became asymmetrical. Schemes for picturesque

Top The second pavilion added to Cressbrook provided a new entrance to the complex. Entry is via a porch in antis in the centre of the elevation. The kitchen block and offices can be seen to the right.

Above left The original section of the house was described in 1849 by Mary McConnel, wife of its builder, as 'vertical slab and shingle verandah cottage'. The shingle roof soon gave way to patented English iron tiles which were replaced by the present iron in 1983.

Left The square verandah posts are lightly stop chamfered and the split slab walls are painted. The elegant windows slide horizontally.

villas abound in early nineteenth century pattern books, as they do in J. C. Loudon's numerous publications. However, such stylistic subtleties were not yet for settlers in remote places, like northern New South Wales, for example, before it was Queensland, inland some hundreds of kilometres on the Brisbane River.

Here stands **Cressbrook** as testimony to the use of local materials and building habits, which even by this early stage had become an Australian tradition. Cressbrook overlooks river flats to the north, and its old pleasure garden is dominated by tall bunya pines, a feature of so many colonial gardens in New

Left The house seen from the large yard around which all the station buildings are built. A tall bunya pine planted by David McConnel dominates the group.

A remarkable feature in Queensland is the robust use of timber. Here at Cressbrook it is used to support a header tank for the homestead. From its beginnings in 1841, the property grew sporadically, with construction always in local timber.

The garden front of the complex looks out over the floodplain of the Brisbane River. This pavilion was altered earlier this century by Robin Dods who added the attic balcony. The shingles are laid over corrugated iron.

The complex seen across the old kitchen garden from the east is dominated by the shingled bungalow pavilion. On the left is the original 1841 house.

South Wales and Queensland. The original section of the house is only one room deep with a broad verandah across the front and a skillion of rooms across the back.

The house is of vertical split hardwood slabs, seated in a ground plate and held together by a top plate supported by posts at the corners and at each aperture. All rooms open on to the timber-floored verandah, and although the rooms have interconnecting doors the verandah is in effect the principal corridor. There are french doors opening to the verandah, and the wide windows are small-paned and slide horizontally. The roof was shingled but was soon covered in patent English iron tiles, the first form of iron roofing to be used in Australia, which appeared in the late 1830s. These survived on Cressbrook until 1983 but have now been replaced.

The interior is typical of the early houses in Queensland where cedar was abundant: the walls and ceilings are lined horizontally with broad boards of local cedar butted together with a delicate screwbead. Never painted or papered, this gives the interiors a quality which is unique. It is like climbing into an old cedar cupboard and closing the door. The

The service yard behind the house is flanked on the west by the slab kitchen, pantry and station offices. Some surviving iron tiles can still be seen on the back of the original section of the complex.

Like nearly all homesteads Cressbrook is really a series of pavilions linked together with verandahs and fences. The original house was only one room deep, with a verandah along the front and skillion rooms at the back.

At the western end of the large station yard is the chapel designed by the Edwardian architect Robin Dods and built in 1902. The house itself is the principal building in what amounts to a village centred on the station yard.

The entrance porch to the family chapel illustrates Dods' imaginative use of locally available timber. It has a rustic simplicity well suited to its environment.

doors are six-panelled of the same wood, and the interiors are dark, cool and glowing with the rich grain of the cedar.

At right angles at the back are the domestic quarters and offices. These have a loft and contain kitchen, pantry, station office, and so on. They are gabled, built of vertical split slab and are more primitive in detail, with simple ledged doors, and compare to the kitchen block at Durham Hall described in the previous chapter.

Cressbrook, commenced by David McConnel in 1841, was an important property and rather like other large stations it

grew and grew. Construction was always in wood, however. The house is the principal building in a small village set out around a large rectangular yard, with the chapel dominating the western end. In 1850 a large bungalow pavilion was built to the right of the earlier house and provided a new entrance to the homestead from the west. As well as the new entrance hall it also had a drawing room, but the dining room remained in the old house and was reached via the verandahs. This pavilion was later altered by Queensland's great Edwardian architect, Robin Dods (1868–1920), to provide attics. Dods also de-

signed the chapel in 1902. Across the garden to the west is Cressbrook Cottage, another bungalow, built later as a dower house. Its construction is timber framed with brick infilling, or nogging, all protected by a deep verandah. It, like the old house, looks out to the north over the river flats.

In areas settled for a longer period, gentlemen and their families now began to think of building houses with fashionable villa fronts, and in Tasmania Thomas Archer, rather like his brother Joseph at nearby Panshanger, completed his estate by building a handsome front to his house.

The dining room in the old house. Floor, walls and ceiling are lined with cedar and the room gives the impression of being inside an old cedar cupboard. Such rooms are a feature of early Queensland houses.

Left *The front hall in the bungalow pavilion, broken by a columned screen, is lined with cedar and beautifully detailed. The scale of this wing contrasts with that of the earlier house.*

Right *The sitting room is one of the rooms refinished by R.S. Dods in a most imaginative way.*

Over Cressbrook from the river flats. Low-spreading roofs, deep verandahs, figtrees, bunya and hoop pines are all characteristic of the early Queensland homestead. The half-timbered Cressbrook Cottage can be seen on the right.

The old section of **Woolmers** is wooden brick nogged and weatherboarded with a large hipped roof and deep flagged verandahs. When this section of the house was built in 1818 Tasmania was just as remote as the Brisbane River was thirty years later, and in its way it is not dissimilar to Cressbrook. It is what the settler could sensibly build using local materials in the wilderness, and Thomas Archer, like David McConnel at Cressbrook, chose to build a bungalow.

Thomas Archer prospered on the South Esk River, and his children were well educated.

His son William went to England to study architecture and became the first Tasmanian-born architect. When in 1842 he returned from his training in London and Newcastle, one of his first tasks was to aggrandise his father's house. He chose to build a fashionable Italian villa front on the timber bungalow. Basically the addition consists of a large front hall with handsome drawing and dining rooms disposed at right angles to each other on either side. There is an Italianate porch below a small tower which contains a bedroom above the hall. The plain end gable wall

of the drawing room on the right is relieved by a blind arch and a broken pediment. The roof is broken into three, with gabled slated roofs over the principal apartments at right angles and a pyramidal roof over the tower, all above boxed eaves. There are elaborate Italianate chimneys which also replaced the earlier stacks on the bungalow — its one concession to modernisation. The sash windows are up-to-date plate glass, and the brick walls are plastered as ashlar with rusticated quoins.

Inside the large hall a door at the end leads into the old house and on the left into the

Left *An avenue of poplars leads to the elaborate dowelled gate in the walled garden before the house.*

Below *Homesteads are in effect villages. Woolmers is seen above the South Esk River. To the right is the horse-driven pumphouse built in the 1840s which pumped water up to the header tank above the store.*

Left *The villa front and carriage circle before the house. In the centre is a cast-iron fountain from Colebrookdale purchased for the property in 1864.*

Below left *A feature of Woolmers are its estate cottages. Pictured here is a picturesque cojoined group which relate closely to similar structures in England.*

Below *The gardener's house is more consciously a cottage* ornée. *Variation was the order for such buildings.*

Left *Detail of a window shutter in the earlier woolshed. The shutter is hung on hand-forged straps and gudgeons. All is in local hardwood.*

The remarkable weatherboarded Georgian vernacular woolshed at Woolmers is probably the oldest in Australia. It dates to c.1815.

The symmetrical stables and coach-house built in 1847 is in the vernacular Georgian tradition. Its walls are roughcast.

Left *The house courtyard with the original weatherboarded verandahed house on the right and at the end the kitchen block added in 1847.*

service passage with the staircase to the bedroom above. On the right, the drawing room is distinguished by a Grecian chimneypiece with caryatids similar to the drawing room chimneypiece at Panshanger. But it is the dining room that is the most handsome room. The wall opposite the windows is broken into three blind arcades: the larger, balancing, arcades take the matching mahogany sideboards; in the centre smaller arch is a door leading into the service passage behind. The end wall of the dining room contains the chimneybreast, which carries a handsome black marble Italianate chimneypiece and is balanced by arched recesses with fitted bookcases. Much of the furnishing in the principal rooms is that chosen by William Archer: the crested oak furniture survives in the hall, handsome rosewood furniture and curtains in the drawing room, and mahogany furniture and red flock wallpaper in the dining room.

In the plasterwork throughout this part of the house are the fashionable papier mâché enrichments from C. F. Bielefeld in London. In a way, all the fashionable things a young architect would have selected in the early Victorian period are represented here. It was probably the most advanced house of its day, a trendsetter.

Woolmers was a big estate, and much of its enhancement was done by William Archer. There was a pleasure garden with handsome gateways, fountain and smoking pavilion. There were estate cottages and a Gothic lodge, all disposed among the earlier vernacular outbuildings on a lovely site above the South Esk River.

Above *The front hall is a very intact early Victorian room. The oak furniture is original to this room, which is unusually spacious for a colonial front hall.*

The service passage which runs across the back of the dining room is screened from the front of the house by an arched doorway and bat wing doors.

The drawing room survives very much as originally furnished. Only the wallpaper, frieze and picture rail are Edwardian alterations. The original paper was green and gold. The suite of Brazilian rosewood furniture, the body and border carpet and rarest of all, the gilt cornice poles together with the valance and curtains, survive.

Left *The dining room retains its original mahogany furniture and a red flock wallpaper put up in 1859. Originally the walls were painted blue. The body of the lath and plaster ceiling has been battened as much for safety as taste, and the carpet is a Victorian replacement.*

Above *The early Victorian crimson tabaret curtains in the drawing room with their bullion fringe and moiré valance. The papier mâché in the cornice was purchased in London at Jackson & Son in 1859.*

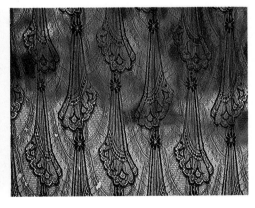

Far left *The Victorian baroque flock wallpaper in the dining room was purchased at Simpson's in London in February 1859.*

Left *The lace undercurtains in the drawing room are an Edwardian replacement.*

Right *Probably the best Italian villa design of the early Victorian period, Rosedale looks out over its walled terrace to well-kept countryside. It is the design of James Blackburn, very much inspired by the writings of J. C. Loudon.*

Below right *Blackburn added a tall loggia across the front of the original house built in 1828. At the end is the entrance to the house itself.*

Bottom *The villa as first seen from the old carriage drive sits against distant hills and looks out to the east over fertile river flats. The old pleasure garden is on the right and behind Blackburn's stable block.*

Another Tasmanian house to be aggrandised in the early Victorian period is **Rosedale** on the Elizabeth River. The first house built at Rosedale in 1828 by the Yorkshireman John Leake was a typical four-roomed verandahed cottage, a storey and a half high, three bays wide by two bays deep, with front and back halls and four rooms with french doors at the front opening on to the flagged verandah which encircled the house. At the sides, detached and set slightly back, were balancing gabled wings which ran back linked by a wall at the rear to form a yard. They housed the kitchen offices, storehouses and stables. It is a Palladian composition seen at many colonial houses, such as Wickford and Clarendon.

Leake prospered, and in 1847 he engaged the notable James Blackburn (1803–54), an architect who had been transported for forgery but had distinguished himself as an architect in the colonial administration, gained his pardon and at this date was living in the Midlands. Blackburn was a true early Victorian architect whose Tasmanian work is characterised by boldness and striving for effect. This he certainly achieved at Rosedale, turning the house from a cottage into a fashionable Italianate villa.

Blackburn cleverly replaced the verandah by a tall loggia with a small tower in front of the old entrance, which was closed up and replaced by two small windows. In front of the left-hand gabled wing he built a two-storeyed hip-roofed pavilion, and at the junction of the new loggia and pavilion a tower was built to dominate the design and add a feature that became a hallmark of the Italianate style for the rest of the nineteenth century. The house is built on a slope, raised at the front. This

Left *The large service yard behind the house is bounded on one side by the extensive stable building with its return wing which still houses the family coach.*

advantage was further played up by Blackburn who created a gravelled terrace before the house, edging it with a curving wall, so that the villa looks out over the rich river flats in a most picturesque way and when seen from the old carriage road was a most remarkable piece of antipodean theatre. Behind the house an outer yard of farm buildings was built, dominated by Blackburn's imposing stables and coach-house on the north. Such a design, as indeed most of Blackburn's designs were, was undoubtedly influenced by Loudon's *Encyclopaedia*. The variety of treatments of the windows, the massing, the enhancement of

the setting, all can be traced to Loudon.

Entry to the house is by the original front steps under the small tower, then along the loggia to the main door below the tower. This leads into a square vestibule with elaborate plasterwork and asymmetrically arranged openings. An arched leadlighted window looks out on to the front terrace, with the doorway to the drawing room beyond it on the left. Opposite, a door leads to a cloakroom and lavatory – an early instance of the technological advances of the period. To the right a door leads to the staircase and behind, in the same wall as the main door entry into

The dining room was formed by architect James Blackburn from two rooms of the 1828 house. The french doors are surviving features of the original building. The wallpaper is a reproduction of a design by G. F. Bodley of 1867.

Above left Looking from the original water closet door across the front hall to the dining room formed within the walls of the original house. The joinery is cedar from New South Wales.

Blackburn's drawing room is an unusually elaborate colonial room. The plasterwork is rich and although the character is Italianate, the detail is Greek. The chandelier and Stoddart piano are original furnishings.

Right The so-called painted room in the original section of the house was once painted in Etruscan mural decoration. The room has elaborate fitted cedar bookcases and retains its chair rail. The portrait is that of Charles Henry Leake who succeeded his father at Rosedale in 1865.

the old house, into the dining room formed from two of its rooms. The staircase leads by an elaborate archway to a dim vestibule on the first floor of the tower. Stairs lead to the top of the tower, and there are tripartite arched windows in its north wall. A further archway leads to the bedrooms above the drawing room on a slightly higher level. This remarkable chamber was once papered with an elaborate Gothic paper in red and stone. The high point of the house, however, is the drawing room. This lofty chamber looks out via a bay window which breaks forward on to a terrace. The ceiling of the room is coffered and plastered in a most elaborate way. Its detail, like that of the bay window which has Doric pilasters, is Grecian, but the total effect is Italianate and early Victorian. Rosedale is perhaps the *beau idéal* of the early Victorian villa in Australia.

Left *The apparently Regency design of Rhodes is in fact the product of a long building period. The section to the right of centre was built first, probably in the late 1820s, the rest, on the site of an earlier cottage, not until considerably later.*

Below *The stable block is not dissimilar to that at nearby Woolmers and could well date to the 1840s.*

Bottom *The stable block has a skillion at the back which provides a shearing shed.*

A neighbouring house to Woolmers is **Rhodes**, originally the property of Thomas Walker who was granted the land in 1818. Unlike Woolmers, the culmination of Rhodes was the completion of a design that would seem to have commenced in the late 1820s. Walker also had land on the Parramatta River in New South Wales where he built a verandahed cottage. On the South Esk River the house is ostensibly a Regency villa, its symmetrical facade broken by a central three-sided bay with pilastered corners projecting forward and balanced by single-storeyed three-sided bays with casements above breast panels, which with their full shutters give the effect of french doors. Three-sided bays are on each return end of the house, and the whole is surmounted by a boxed-eave hipped roof which picks up the three principal bays.

Rhodes is approached by a carriage drive which edges a pleasure garden laid out in beds bordered by box hedging and opens into a large carriage circle before the house. There is a handsome stable block behind the house and a cottage that is almost a single-storeyed version of the main house.

Before the house is a wonderfully intact Victorian pleasure garden laid out in a geometrical pattern edged with mature box hedging.

Entry into Rhodes is straight into the broad and spacious stair hall which takes up the whole of the centre bay of the house. The cedar staircase runs across the hall and the ceiling has been battened this century.

A timber pulley wheel in the roof of the stable block behind the main house allows for stores to be hauled into the loft. The shingle battens and split shingles survive intact under the corrugated-iron roof.

Entry to the house is via fanlit double doors, each of single panels, which to some extent give the secret to the date of completion of the house. The unusually broad front hall runs halfway across the house, with the cedar stair climbing the opposite wall. To the left is the drawing room with high ceiling and heavy, early Victorian plasterwork; opposite, looking out towards the river, is the dining room where the ceiling is lower and the windows have shutter boxes, as do the drawing room windows. It seems the stair hall and the right-hand two-storey section of the house was built in the 1820s, but the balancing half of the house was not built until later without any apparent external modification to the early design. Rhodes is said to have been designed partly by Mrs Walker, who was a daughter of John Blaxland of Newington on the Parramatta River. Her father's house was built in 1832, and the general form of the two houses is not dissimilar. Rhodes is an example of the continuing Georgian tradition in Australia.

The dining room is in the oldest section of the house. The windows have shutter boxes and in the left-hand window the shutters are closed against the glass.

The beautiful early Victorian brass knocker on the cedar front door of Rhodes. The fanlit, single-panelled double doors help to date the house's completion to sometime in the 1840s.

Left *Hill River seen across its fine twentieth-century garden. On the right is the wing added by Jack Evans in 1927.*

By the late 1840s the Clare Valley of South Australia was sufficiently settled for gentlemen to build decorative cottages. At **Hill River** in 1849 Robert Robinson built a stone gabled verandahed cottage, four bays by two, with a slated roof. There are shuttered french doors under the verandah, and the main door is fitted with a classical doorcase rendered and finished in sand paint. A certain Gothic character is played up by the parapeted gables and the blind Gothic arches on the chimneystacks. Otherwise the detail is con-ventional enough. There are twelve-paned sash windows and four-panelled doors, and a surviving chimneypiece is in cedar and classi-cal in concept.

In 1927 Hill River was added to quite con-siderably at the side by Adelaide architect Jack Evans, in the process creating some remark-able colonial revival interiors.

Beyond the house are stone stables which are part of an original stable yard. The hand-some stable building has balancing gables to break its facade.

The stable block and carriage house is in fact one side of a complex of farm buildings. Like the house itself, the influence of the Gothic revival is evident in the gables in this otherwise balanced vernacular design.

The group of station buildings beyond the house looks out over the beautiful pastoral landscape of the Clare Valley in South Australia.

The house has parapeted gables and the chimneys are enriched by blind Gothic arches. The verandah is a late Victorian replacement.

Left *Hartwood is a verandahed bungalow, one room deep surrounded by deep verandahs. It was built by Patrick Brougham in the Riverina, its long, low styling epitomising the Australian rural tradition.*

Right *The simple design is enriched by elegant sash windows, bracketed verandah posts and a simplified chinoiserie balustrade.*

Below *The slab walls are hidden by plaster, the windows have architraves and there is a timber plinth to the wall. The main door, which is off-centre, has an naive classical doorcase.*

Despite the stylistic preoccupations of gentlemen settlers in certain places, the Riverina area of New South Wales was still very remote in the early Victorian period. Here, at **Hartwood**, Patrick Brougham built a bungalow in the best tradition of the Australian countryside. Brougham was a nephew of Lord Brougham, one of the chief legal luminaries of the nineteenth century. He and his brother John had come to seek their fortune in Australia, and both married sisters of the pioneering Kennedy family of Boorowa.

Long and low, one room deep, with an encircling verandah under the same main roof, Hartwood is not dissimilar to Cressbrook with the verandah as the principal means of access, except that it has more architectural pretensions. It has large twelve-paned sash windows with external architraves, and the wide front door is marked by a somewhat primitive classical doorcase. But perhaps its most interesting feature is that its slab walls are hidden from view by a coating of lath and plaster. In fact, it pretends to be a masonry house, the soft plastered walls protected by its deep verandahs. Inside, the walls were treated in the same way. The ceilings are pine, and there are simple wooden chimneypieces. Away from the rainforests of the coast, the principal workable building timber in the western districts of New South Wales was cypress or Murray pine. White-ant resistant, it has allowed many early houses to survive.

Right *The pine bush poles which serve as rafters to the verandah retain their bark and the shingle battens are in fact split, an almost deliberately rustic finish.*

Far right *The walls are plastered inside and there is a dado of beaded cypress pine boarding and fitted cupboards beside chimneybreasts. Like the interiors of many Queensland houses, the interior linings are left unpainted.*

The verandah is supported on square stop chamfered posts, and between there is a balustrade of the simplest Chinese Chippendale form often found in colonial buildings. One intriguing detail is the verandah ceiling. While it is normal for such houses not to have linings to verandahs, and to reveal the underside of shingle battens and split shingles, it is not so usual for the bush pole rafters to be left with their bark on. This is perhaps a deliberate touch of picturesque rusticity.

Later owners added to and rebuilt the original service rooms of the house, and behind the house is a group of three brick buildings which with the old house form a courtyard. The dining room and smoking room date from 1907, as do the stables and manager's house and other brick outbuildings. The old house still looks out from its sand hill and over its mature garden.

The industrial revolution was to provide another means for settlers to have a house. If they were not prepared to cut down the cedar trees, gum trees and cypress pine and fashion the house from what they found virtually on the site, prosperous settlers were now able to buy a ready-made prefabricated house from a catalogue. Houses were available in timber, cast iron and even papier mâché.

The typical Edwardian chimneypiece in the dining room added in 1907 is Georgian inspired. The dining room was but one of several additions made at that time.

The return of the verandah has been filled in with a weatherboarded addition. Entry to the house is through a wide front door fitted with a somewhat primitive classical doorcase.

The Edwardian dining room has a bay window which typifies the broken plan form of the Federation period. The ceiling is boarded and a chair rail symbolises the revived interest in eighteenth-century taste. This revival of Georgian taste is further strengthened by the Chippendale-style dining chairs.

Above right *Wingecarribee is a prefabricated iron house from Hemmings of Bristol. It was built in 1857. The house has two principal fronts at right angles. This is the entrance front; the other faces the garden.*

Houses in all these materials are known to have been sent to Australia, but few seem to have survived. None is known in papier mâché, and few are known in other materials. Woodlands in Victoria, with its cast-iron windows, is a notable timber survivor, and **Wingecarribee** in the southern highlands of New South Wales, a notable cast-iron example. John Oxley, the explorer and Surveyor-General of New South Wales, was given the land in 1815, but it was his Australian-educated son Henry who erected the house in 1857. Oxley chose his house from the portfolio of designs of *Hemming's*

Patent Improved Portable Houses manufactured in Bristol, and available from the Melbourne & Colonial House Investment Co.

Wingecarribee is sited against hills and looks out to the east from the plateau on which it sits, its garden marked by the inevitable bunya pine. The house seems strangely American, yet its design is ostensibly Italianate. It is single-storey, rectangular plan, its roof hidden by a blind cast-iron parapet surmounted by classical urns. There are two fronts at right angles, one facing the garden and the other providing the entrance to the house. The frame is in the form of

Detail of the construction. Except for the shutters and the verandah framing, everything is iron.

Right *The garden front of the house looks out to the east, its site dominated by a bunya pine, a tree that often marks the colonial house.*

The plate glass sash windows are fitted inside with shutter boxes; the shutter panels themselves are enriched with papier mâché. The external louvre shutters are closed against the window glass.

Right *Because of the thickness of the walls the shutter boxes protrude into the room. The double drawing room survives with much of its Brazilian rosewood suite. At the end is a Victorian holland blind with a decorative lace insert.*

classical iron pilasters which mark the bays of the house and are infilled with vertical corrugated-iron sheets. The timber-framed verandah was built along both fronts, although in the catalogue the verandah is shown only on the garden front. The rest of the detail is conventional enough. The large shuttered sash windows are timber with plate glass, and inside there are shutter boxes and breast panels. Because of the thinness of the walls, these protrude into the rooms. Entry is via double doors into a broad hall which by means of an archway leads into a skylit central hall. The ceilings and walls are timber-framed

and boarded, the latter lined with scrim and papered and fitted with conventional Italianate joinery sent as part of the package. Papier mâché is used to enrich the ceilings and the doors.

The drawing room and sitting room, en suite with large connecting folding doors, and the dining room are on the left of the hall and look out over the garden front. They are fitted with marble chimneypieces which came with the package, white in the drawing and sitting rooms, black in the dining room.

The house forms a 'U' on plan with a central courtyard now covered.

All the ceilings are boarded and in the principal rooms there are papier mâché enrichments. Here the original cornice poles, dining table and chairs survive.

Left The central hall has a skylight and battened timber ceiling enriched with papier mâché. The doors are six-panelled.

By the 1850s the western plains of New South Wales were being opened for settlement. A rare and intact settler's house of this first wave of settlement is **The Springs** on the Little River built by a Scottish settler, Thomas Baird, in 1858. The house at The Springs is a weatherboarded bungalow of low proportion and is unusual for the main double-pile section of the house being gabled. This is encircled by a timber-floored verandah supported on square stop chamfered posts, the roof of lesser pitch, under which at each end are skillion rooms brought forward on the front and back elevations so that the verandahs are *in antis*. This is a sophistication common to a number of colonial bungalows and was perhaps first realised by John Macarthur with his alterations to Elizabeth Farm at Parramatta in 1826.

The two elevations of the house provide an entrance front and a garden front. The offices and kitchen are off to the side linked by a covered way. Under the verandah each elevation is the same: five bays wide with windows balancing a central doorway. The sash windows are twelve-paned, and the doors are

Watercolour of The Springs shortly after its construction. The painting is by Thomas Baird's daughter Kennedy who died in 1859. In the right of the painting can be seen a bark-roofed building which has since disappeared.

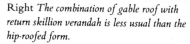

A similar view to that taken in the watercolour. In the foreground the bachelors' quarters have been built and the roofs are covered in corrugated iron.

Right The combination of gable roof with return skillion verandah is less usual than the hip-roofed form.

four-panelled of unusual high-waisted proportion. Wide beaded boards line the verandah ceiling, and all is painted except for the cedar doors and sashes which are varnished.

The central hall, which divides the house inside, is broken by a pine screen and on each side are two rooms. The dining and drawing rooms look out over the garden; the other two rooms are bedrooms. Wide beaded boards line the walls, similar to those at Cressbrook, but here they have been painted.

These are undoubtedly pine, and only the cedar fittings, doors and chimneypieces are left polished.

While the house is of dressed timber, the kitchen and other offices, stables and barns which form the considerable complex are of slab construction either sawn or split, some placed vertically and some in drop log construction. There are bush pole columns, rafters and joists.

In the garden before the house is a water

race from the springs which give the house its name. This is connected to a header tank which feeds a bath house in the garden. A late 1850s watercolour by a daughter of the house shows how little the complex has changed. Except for ubiquitous iron covering the shingled roofs and the building of the gabled bachelors' quarters, it is much the same. Many settlers' houses of this type existed, but many have been aggrandised or considerably altered. The Springs is a rare survival.

Under the verandah the windows are larger and the sashes are left unpainted. The french doors are a later alteration. Squatters chairs with movable leg rests help furnish the verandah.

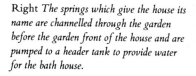

Right The springs which give the house its name are channelled through the garden before the garden front of the house and are pumped to a header tank to provide water for the bath house.

While the house is of dressed weatherboards, the numerous outhouses and sheds which make up the considerable group of buildings are all of slab or pole construction. These buildings are of horizontal slab construction, pole in the foreground, sawn slab in the background, held to the posts by cleats nailed in position.

Above right *A barrel vault of corrugated iron roofs the covered way that links the house to the kitchen at the side.*

Right *The top-hung ledged shutters in the laundry are fashioned from locally found cypress pine.*

The bath house in the garden is raised on stumps and walled with vertical sawn slabs held in position by cleats fitted to the top and bottom plates.

Right *The kitchen survives in near original condition. Like most colonial kitchens there is no ceiling and the underside of the roofing, in this case corrugated iron, is smoked black from the constantly burning fire.*

Far right *The English steam engine was purchased in 1907 for £250.00. It was made by Marshall & Sons of Gainsborough and was used until 1956 for general farm work and for running the overhead gear used for shearing.*

The central hall is broken by a panelled screen of stained cypress pine. The walls and ceiling are lined with painted wide-beaded pine boards. The four-panelled doors of cedar are polished.

Above left *The woolshed is part iron and part slab. Corrugated iron was first used for roofing but was increasingly used as sidings for outhouses. The shingle battens can still be seen on the left-hand gable.*

Left *The dining room overlooks the garden. Like the internal doors the twelve-paned sash windows are polished. Cedar cornice poles survive at the windows.*

Below *The sitting room retains some of its parlour furniture, its central cedar loo table and its fine cedar sofa with arms and backboards carved with swans. The cedar chimneypiece is one of four in the house.*

One of the bedrooms at the front of the house survives with its four-poster bed and large cedar chest of drawers.

Opposite page Of all roof shapes this form is the most common in Australia. Here painted 'tile red', Gracemere looks out from its lush tropical garden to the waterway that gives it its name.

Within the garden that surrounds the house are sixteen different coloured bougainvilleas. The house is heavy with this vine which is carried across the front on a pergola.

In the remote north of the country, in what was soon to become a separate colony named Queensland in 1859, the Archer family built their house in the wilderness. This is **Gracemere**, near the Fitzroy River inland from Rockhampton, overlooking a lagoon which gives it its name. It too is a bungalow.

Colin Archer, who built Gracemere for his family of pioneering brothers, was trained as a naval architect. Although the single-pile plan in the form of an 'L' with the encircling verandah would seem to relate in form more to the experience of other settlers like David McConnel at Cressbrook, it is the scale of Gracemere that is so different, and the problem was getting split slabs of ironbark (one of the *Eucalyptus* species) of the required length. The innovation is the breaking of the walls at door head height by a horizontal plate, below which in each bay there is a door and casement window. The doors are four-panelled and open out, and the windows are shuttered. Above, in each bay, is a ventilation opening in the form of a ledged door. To overcome the problem of timber length, for the back wing of the house, which includes the dining room, another species of timber was used, sawn into wide beaded planks, which were fitted between the timber frame. By this means no lining was necessary.

In the interior the walls of the front of the house are lined with vertical cedar boards and left unpainted. The ceilings are also sheeted with dark cedar boards, contrasting with the light colour of the pine floor. Only the external face of the casements is painted. There is nothing moulded or trimmed, and this gives the house a robustness not found in other houses. The scale is considerable for a slab house. The ceilings are 3.65 metres (12 feet) high, and the main room is 9.75 x 4.55 metres (32 x 15 feet). The present appearance of the house owes much to Mrs Robert Archer and her daughter-in-law Mrs Alister Archer, who decorated the house earlier this century with furniture and chimneypieces hand-carved from Nordic illustrations. These, combined with the robust quality of the house and the satin curtains and Belgian rugs, give the interiors a rare individual quality.

From the deep verandahs heavy with bougainvillea (there are sixteen different colours in the garden) you look out over a mature flower garden which runs down to the lake. Many of the plants were brought from Sydney's Botanic Gardens when Charles Archer laid out the garden in the 1860s. Gracemere is a tropical paradise, its site on a

Above left *Under the verandah the construction of the house is revealed: split slab walls, adzed columns and plates and exposed rafters.*

Far left *The women of the house have carved a remarkable chimneypiece, reflecting not only the Scandinavian experience of the family, but also the growing nationalism of Australia.*

Left *It was difficult to obtain slabs long enough for Gracemere's high ceilings, so the walls have been ingeniously broken at door head height.*

The dining room is in the side return of the house which is constructed differently and appears slightly later. This is the only painted room in the house. The sideboard is Edwardian, carved by the women of the house with a distinct Scandinavian influence. The table is early Victorian.

Left The rear verandah at the internal corner of the building gives access to the sitting room on the left and beyond the principal bedroom. Above each window in the front of the house is a ventilation shutter.

The great sitting room at Gracemere is lined with cedar with a floor of colonial pine. Only the casements are painted. Carved furniture in the Nordic style is a feature of this room.

peninsula marked by towering palms and Leichhardt trees.

The educated taste that creates a house like Gracemere shows how in the wilderness an elegant house could be built from what is readily to hand. Its almost deliberate rusticity would have appealed to a gentleman educated in the first quarter of the nineteenth century. It could be seen as a rustic habitation, referred to as a *cottage ornée*.

In more settled districts like the Goulburn Plains what a gentleman could build in 1858 was little different from the choices available in any of the provinces of the United Kingdom at that time. Here there were architects and builders on hand to build what was illustrated in architectural journals and published in pattern books. Unlike the earlier houses we have seen, which were broadly a synthesis of ideas found in pattern books, **Springfield** is a good example of a house built directly from one. The house was built by a second-generation Australian, William Faithfull, on land he had had since 1827. Similar to what we have seen at Woolmers, it was a grand front to mark the culmination of its proprietor's success.

Faithfull grafted his Italianate villa on to an existing house, part of which was picturesque Gothic in character with steeply pitched roofs and barge boards and beyond that the original house which was vernacular Georgian. Seen in side elevation the house is rather like three volumes of architecture. The Italianate design Faithfull chose first appeared in Loudon's

The sitting room of Gracemere glimpsed from under the pergola which carries the bougainvillea vines across the front of the house. Family portraits in gilt mounts look down on the rich and dark interior, decorated early this century by Mrs Robert Archer and her daughter-in-law Mrs Alister Archer.

Architectural Magazine in 1836 described as a 'Design for a Suburban Villa with Two Acres of Ground. The design was contributed by Edward Buckton Lamb (1805–69), an English architect best known for his country houses and churches, the latter in a rather 'deposed' Gothic which made him unpopular with the Ecclesiological Society. The design was again published by Loudon in 1838 in his *Suburban Gardener and Villa Companion* described as 'A Suburban Villa with the House in the Italian Style and the Ground laid out in Picturesque Manner'. So the design was twenty years old when Faithfull decided to adopt it. The house built is somewhat simplified from the published design and probably had something to do with cost. It is also compromised by the fact that it backs on to an existing house and is not a villa in the round and has no basement offices. The main change is the tower which, as built, is square, not octagonal as suggested by Lamb; and as if to suit colonial habits the

Left *The design on which Springfield is based first appeared in Loudon's Architectural Magazine in 1836. The villa is built in front of two earlier buildings which can be seen at the side. Originally the roof was shingled.*

Below *The principal staircase in the house is constructed of cedar. Before 1951 the staircase was screened from the outer hall by double doors.*

In contrast to the Italianate style of the house, the coach-house, built of the same materials, is Gothic in style and its form may well have devolved from a published architectural design.

Opposite page *The Italian villa front of Springfield, based on a published design in Loudon, is seen over the clipped hedgerows that surround its extensive gardens.*

Springfield seen across the pleasure garden. The house is the focus of a large estate, screened by a belt of mature trees and including both a pleasure garden and kitchen gardens.

The large drawing room with its white Carrara marble chimneypiece looks out through french doors to the extensive pleasure garden at the side of the house. Before 1951 these doors had normal sidelights.

open terraces are sheltered by light concave awnings with cast-iron supports instead of the open masonry balustraded balconies in the published design.

A verandahed porch with french doors with sidelights is the major feature at the side of the house, replacing the elaborate chimney-stack and window suggested by Lamb. Lamb shows a window above the drawing room chimneypiece where a mirror would normally be, a trick device beloved of many early Victorian architects. Barry used this device at the Reform Club in 1837, and it became very fashionable.

Springfield is built of dark sandstock brick with stone dressings. Entry is made via a porch into a square front hall. To the left is the library and to the right the entrance to the drawing room which is via a bay that breaks forward in the room. The chimneypiece is opposite, and the side or right-hand wall is taken up by a set of french doors with side lights changed in 1951 to sash windows which look out on to a verandahed porch to the extensive pleasure garden beside the house. The staircase hall is opposite the front door and before 1951 was separated from the front hall by an inner set of doors. Behind the library and off the stair hall is the dining room. The staircase leads to the first floor, where there are four principal bedrooms. The house is well detailed with large small-paned sash windows with semi-circular heads, good cedar joinery, marble chimneypieces and strong early

Victorian plasterwork.

Like Panshanger the house sits at the centre of a large estate with all the appurtenances that go with it. The house is set in a belt of trees, and the drive skirts the extensive pleasure garden, beyond which are the kitchen gardens. The tower of the house is seen above this first garden and you are brought to a sweep of gravel before the porch. Beyond the house is a large quadrangle rather like Cressbrook with the station buildings ranged out around what is virtually a village green. Notable amongst the outbuildings are the estate cottages and the fine picturesque Gothic stables, which still retain their iron tile roof of the type that was once on Cressbrook.

While most influences on Australian architecture up to now had been British, the publication of architectural pattern books allowed for broader influences. One such influence

was the book by the American architect Calvert Vaux (1824–95), *Villas and Cottages*, first published in New York in 1857.

In 1862 Edward Archer, brother of Joseph Archer of Panshanger and Thomas Archer of Woolmers, chose Design No. 19, 'Suburban Villa', as the inspiration for his house at **Northbury** not far from Launceston. The design would seem to have been adapted somewhat. It is simpler and is smaller in scale. Whether his nephew, the architect William Archer, had anything to do with it is not known. The house is an 'L' on plan and wraps around the three-storey tower at the internal corner, from which extends a single-storey arcaded loggia across the right-hand front of the house. The tower is capped by a pyramidal roof, whereas the remainder of the roof is gabled with deep overhanging bracketed eaves in the Italianate mode.

It is at once more American than English. The plan has been simplified, with the stair in the front hall and only two principal rooms on the ground floor, whereas in the Vaux design there are three. The design, being double pile, has a range of rooms across the back. Exterior walls are stuccoed, and while the design is very up to date its details are old-fashioned. The sashes on the ground floor and the casements upstairs are small paned, and inside the house has good cedar joinery and plasterwork which could well be earlier. The chimneypieces in the bedrooms suggest the colonial Georgian period rather than the fashionable Italianate.

Vaux was just as influential as Loudon, and country houses like Mount Pleasant in New South Wales and Longerenong in northwestern Victoria would seem to have been inspired by his book.

Right *As a young man Edward Archer had visited America. Whether this influenced him to choose an American design for the house he later built is unclear, but Northbury is an early example of the influence of American architecture in Australia.*

Below *The staircase is typically of cedar and of geometrical design. The square balusters are replacements.*

Below right *Despite its up-to-date appearance, under the loggia and inside the house reverts to more old-fashioned details. Edward Archer died early in 1862 so the house is most probably earlier.*

One of the bedrooms at Northbury is intriguingly and imaginatively papered with prints and illustrations from late Victorian journals. The chimneypiece shown at left is late Georgian in style.

Left One of the bow windows used to advantage on the exterior of the house lights the dining room.

One of the best and most assured of early Victorian architects was the Melbourne-based Leonard Terry (1825–84). His was a large practice, and he was responsible for many buildings not only in Victoria but also in New Zealand and Tasmania. He is best remembered as the designer of Italian *palazzo*-style urban buildings, notable amongst which is the Melbourne Club of 1858 and the Bank of New Zealand, Auckland, of 1865. Although the Italian *palazzo* was his chosen style, he did work in Gothic for churches, and probably his best country house, **Norwood**, was built in this style in 1863–65 for the self-made grazier Alfred Joyce.

Built of local grey basalt, this expensive and well-detailed house makes it a rare example of its style of architecture. Gothic revival, if it was to be properly done, was expensive, it had to be executed in stone, and all its details had to be fully realised. It was much cheaper to run up a house in brick and either finish it with rendered details or cover it entirely in cement with cast details and pretend it was stone. This was all right for Italianate houses but somehow was inexcusable for a Gothic revival building, and following the teaching of Pugin and the English Ecclesiological Society Gothic revival architecture must be truthfully done.

So the steep slated parapeted gables of Norwood, its well-executed stonework, its asymmetry, tall chimneys, casement windows, corbelled oriel window, properly detailed entrance and crenellated parapets make it as good an example of a revived Tudor manor house as you will find in Australia. But as if to remind us that we are in Australia,

Norwood has verandahs, two bays to the left of the porch, three bays to the right, executed in richly detailed Gothic-style woodwork. Alfred Joyce was eventually made insolvent, and probably the cost of building a house like Norwood contributed to his financial problems.

After the 1860s the purity of style that we have seen in houses like Norwood and Northbury somehow starts to wane, and buildings become much more obviously Victorian, style becomes less important, architecture becomes heavier, and there is a certain grittiness about the buildings. Buildings also became more muscular and less fanciful.

Steep parapeted gables, label moulds, crenellated parapets, tall chimneys and Tudor arches are all beautifully carried out in this well-detailed house.

Above left *The full-blown Gothic revival style was rarely used for houses largely due to expense. One exception however is Norwood, designed by the talented Melbourne architect Leonard Terry and built between 1863 and 1865.*

Left *It is only really the verandah that makes Norwood not a totally English revived Tudor manor house. The verandah is well detailed and richly decorated in heavy stop chamfered woodwork.*

Mid Victorian

In 1864 the English architect Robert Kerr (1823–1904) – he was professor of architecture at King's College, London – published *The Gentleman's House,* a book that was to be as influential on the construction of houses during the succeeding two decades as Loudon's encyclopaedia had been in the early Victorian period. Kerr's book included a range of designs, as the rest of its title indicated: *How to Plan English Residences from the Parsonage to the Palace.* This book joined a burgeoning Victorian library that helped gentlemen and their architects to build. We have already mentioned the American book of Calvert Vaux. There were also Wickes' *A Handy Book of Villa Architecture* and later Stevenson's *House Architecture* and Richardson's *The Englishman's House,* just to name a few.

One house whose appearance is similar to those advocated by Kerr is **Mona Vale** in midland Tasmania, although its crispness of detail and quality of materials give it a lightness of character that is more early Victorian in feeling, very much like many of Sir Charles Barry's Italian *palazzo* country houses in England in the 1840s. In design it is a house on the cusp and could well have been treated in the last chapter.

Mona Vale is not an amateur work. It is the *pièce de résistance* of the Tasmanian architect William Archer, whom we have already seen at his father's house, Woolmers. Archer was a gentleman architect, and his limited output was restricted to his family and friends. Mona Vale was built for his brother-in-law, Robert Kermode, in 1864–67; the house is on the site of an earlier Georgian house built by Robert's father, William Kermode, which was taken down.

On its site close to the Blackman River, which had been dammed before the house to form a lake, the belvedere of the Italianate house is first glimpsed through the trees above water as it is approached. The house is reached at the angle, and its two principal fronts come into view as the river is crossed and the carriage road sweeps around, skirting the pleasure garden with its fountain on the left, into the rectangular gravelled forecourt edged with stone balustrading before the house. In the centre of the forecourt is another fountain. It is all very noble. As Kerr advised, the gentleman's house should have 'elegance and importance without ostentation'. The three-storeyed house is built of warm freestone, its Italianate detail of window surrounds to the large sash windows different on each floor, the rusticated quoins, the string courses, the ashlar and the principal cornice all beautifully executed. The plan of the main front section relies on the principle we have seen before in Italian villa designs: the two principal rooms, namely the drawing room and the dining room, are placed at right angles to each other with a break between to mark the entrance. Here it is a recessed front-ispiece marked by venetian windows.

At Mona Vale the tower is set back behind. Above the cornice are hipped roofs of slate, and the tower is topped by a belvedere. An arcaded porch marks the main door, and timber-framed verandahs run from the porch around the house over the flagged terraces on the principal fronts; on the garden front it breaks forward into a three-sided bow centred on the drawing room.

Entry to the house is via a large front hall which has a floor of encaustic tiles and a black marble chimneypiece. Few houses in Australia can boast a fireplace in the hall, and this is perhaps an indication that Mona Vale is more mansion than house. To the right is the dining room and to the left the drawing room. Behind the dining room a corridor provides access to the principal stair which is at the side of the house. Running behind the drawing room are a series of lesser reception rooms, writing room, library, morning room, business room and so on, all reached from a corridor from the hall and screened by a door. This range and the two-storeyed domestic range of pantries, kitchen, scullery, etc., running behind the principal staircase, form a long courtyard behind the house dominated by the tower. The stair is the most disappointing feature, and its position on the main route from the kitchen to dining room is not something that would have been admired by the best Victorian architects, who went to no end of trouble to separate the servants from the family.

The noble dining room was originally decorated in a geometric 'Reckitt's blue' paper set out in bordered panels and surmounted by a classical frieze all in the same blue. The curtains were scarlet rep on gilt poles, and the mahogany and cedar furniture sat on a Turkey carpet. It was very rich. In the balancing drawing room, where the ceiling was enriched with papier mâché, the original grey and gold diapered paper survives as does its gilt fillet. All the doors to the principal rooms have handsome Italianate doorcases.

One of the most interesting spaces in the house is the corridor on the second floor, at the top of the house. It is Georgian in feeling, with a plastered segmental vault and six-

On completion in 1868 Mona Vale was described as 'one of the most handsomely furnished residences in the colonies . . . replete with every comfort and convenience'.

Right *The drawing room is papered in grey with a diapered pattern in gold and the doors are fitted with elaborate Italianate doorcases.*

The fine Victorian conservatory was designed by Archer in 1866 and is contemporary with the house. It curves round to meet the house itself.

The earlier greenhouse was described in 1868 as being '100 feet long and filled with a magnificent display of choice plants in full bloom'.

panelled doors reused from the demolished house. Here the joinery is still grained as oak, and the walls are papered in imitation of blocks of Sienna marble.

Behind the house are several outbuildings and walls from the earlier house and beyond

this again a whole village of estate cottages and outbuildings designed by Archer contemporaneously with the house. On the northern side of the house, stretching back along the rear walls, are a series of detached heated conservatories on a scale unequalled in Australia.

The rear conservatory 30 metres (100 feet) in length would appear to date with the earlier house, and the grander one, which curves around to meet the house, with the construction of the house. Beyond the conservatories is Archer's Gothic revival chapel.

Perricoota is the archetypal two-storeyed house of the mid Victorian period. In elevation and plan form it is like many colonial houses.

A much more typical country house of the 1860s is **Perricoota** on the Murray River in the remote south-west of New South Wales. This is a more conventional two-storeyed brick house of a double-pile plan, five bays wide, with an encircling concave cast-iron

framed verandah on the ground floor over a tile-paved terrace.

The big house is built to the left of the earlier single-pile brick bungalow. Perricoota is Italianate in detail with its brick walls enriched with rendered dressings, quoins and

rustications below bracketed wooden boxed eaves and a slate hipped roof. It is, if you like, a single Italianate pavilion and makes nothing of the picturesque ideas taken up by builders of so many Victorian houses of this style. It is little different in basic concept to houses of the 1830s, such as Streanshalh in Tasmania. It is very much a house with one front, and is an example of colonial Georgian survival in Australia. Although it uses up-to-date sash windows, its shuttered french doors to the verandah still have a margined glazing pattern which would have been quite old-fashioned in the 1860s.

Inside, the central hall, divided by an arch, is tiled, and the large balancing principal rooms have fashionable marble chimneypieces. In the dining room the original cedar furniture survives. The house also boasts a billiard room at the back. The largest room, it has fitted cupboards. It was a room that became increasingly part of country-house life in this period. It was part of the male domain, a curious feature of the Victorian house. At Perricoota the billiard room is balanced on the other side by a cross corridor, a pantry and a schoolroom which looks out to the garden.

Above left *The detail of the house is typically mid Victorian. The cast-iron verandah structure, the terracotta paved terrace and the elaborately moulded front door with its rendered surround are typical.*

Above *The french doors, in contrast to the rest of the detail, are quite old-fashioned. Plate glass had surplanted crown glass by this time and margin bars and elaborate glazing patterns had become unnecessary.*

Left *The house seen across the garden. The early brick bungalow can be seen on the right and to the left the kitchen, at the side of the house.*

Except for the stair, which is cedar, the joinery is painted and is probably pine. Across the back of the house the verandah is two-storeyed, and the first floor bedrooms look out through french doors over the garden running down to the Murray River. The domestic offices are at the side, balancing the earlier bungalow, linked by a corridor behind the dining room. Typically there are cornices downstairs, but upstairs the lath and plaster ceilings are set square to the wall.

Perricoota was built by wealthy Canadian-born graziers Alexander Robertson and John Wagner, who also were principals of the coaching firm of Cobb & Co., and at Perricoota they bred coach horses. In Melbourne Alexander Robertson employed the German-trained architect J. A. B. Koch for his house Ontario (now called Labassa) in 1887, so it is conceivable that Koch designed Perricoota also. Robertson entertained lavishly. The Duke of Edinburgh was entertained at Perricoota in 1868, and the Duke also stayed at Mona Vale where a bed used by him is still to be found, its footboard specially carved with the ducal arms. A royal visit was a considerable accolade for a country house.

A contemporary house in New South Wales which makes much more of the picturesque approach to design is **Frankfield** on the Yass plains. This single-storeyed bungalow was built in 1870 by Francis Rawdon Hume, a second-generation Australian and nephew of the explorer Hamilton Hume.

Here the basic verandahed five-bay-wide double-pile bungalow is used in a picturesque way. The house has two principal elevations and is approached on the angle so that two verandahed elevations are seen, one facing the garden with bow windows on the left, the other with the front door facing the drive. At the other end the verandah returns on to a squat two-storeyed Italianate tower with a pyramidal roof, arched windows and rusticated quoins. Beyond this the picturesque qualities of the ensemble are further played up by a heavily modelled conservatory. The details are conservative enough for their time: elegant wooden verandah, bolection-moulded door panels and heavily detailed front doorcase. Inside the house is similarly typically finished, with four-panelled doors, and the principal rooms on the left look out over the garden. Nothing of the picturesque so successfully played up outside is used inside, and the conservatory can only be reached externally. One yearns for an enfilade of rooms on the cross-axis picking up the tower and culminating in the conservatory – the sort of thing one finds in many English country houses of the time. But no, it suggests that Mr Hume read books like Loudon's, but he was an amateur and did not have the wherewithal to make such a triumph. The tower contains the kitchen on the ground floor and

Frankfield is a picturesque composition: verandahed bungalow, tower and conservatory. Under the verandah on the left are the balanced bay windows of the principal rooms which break into the verandah and look out over the pleasure garden.

The conservatory is an amazing Italianate structure, its design possibly deriving from a pattern book. The detail of the verandah valance is Gothic.

servant's room above. One suspects that ideas developed as the house was built rather than being one total concept and that the exterior composition was all-important. Hume's picturesque taste is further exemplified in the picturesque coach-house and stables, French in character with a quirky mansard roof, which dominates the hill beyond the house. The house and garden are encircled by a picket fence. Below the garden is a lake, on the side of which is a bath house with a plunge bath fed from the lake. Certain luxuries were now considered part of country life, particularly in those areas where European settlement had been established for some time.

Northern New South Wales had become a separate colony, Queensland, in 1859, and the first railway between Ipswich and Grandchester was opened in 1865. In the 1870s, despite the settled nature of the place, the preferred country houses in the region were still bungalows.

Henry Mort (brother of Thomas Sutcliffe Mort) had had land at **Franklyn Vale** since 1849 and had lived in the old slab-built house down under the bunya pines by the creek. But

Frankfield is something of a mid Victorian architectural gallery. Beyond the garden is the coach-house which, in contrast to the Italianate character of the house, is in a quirky French Renaissance style.

Behind the house is the old slab and weatherboard kitchen with its shingle roof still in position. The normal arrangement of colonial cooking can be seen: the open fireplace with hooks for boiling and on the right the brick oven for baking.

The front door is strongly Italianate with balanced pilasters, and with raised panels and bolection moulds to the door panels. The leadlight glazing is probably Edwardian. Frankfield, built on the Yass plains by Francis Rawdon Hume in 1870, successfully utilises elements of the picturesque style on the exterior.

Left The french doors to the main verandah have their kick panels detailed like the front door. The threshold is made of timber.

by 1870 Mort was living in Sydney in some style at Mount Adelaide on top of Darling Point where Babworth House is today. A new large stud-framed weatherboarded bungalow, originally with shingled roofs, was built at Franklyn Vale by his son-in-law, Edward Crace, a retired army officer who, following his marriage to Kate Mort in 1871, acted as Henry Mort's manager. Interestingly, Edward Crace was the grandson of John Gregory Crace, one of the most important decorators of the nineteenth century, his firm being responsible for some of the most significant British country houses. In 1877, Mr and Mrs Edward Crace moved to Gungahleen in what is now the Australian Capital Territory. The house they built was furnished by John G. Crace & Co. of London.

The main block is a double-pile plan five bays wide with a deep timber verandah across the front and down the left-hand side. As if to acknowledge picturesque Victorian taste the verandah did not originally return at the right-hand side, and the drawing room was marked by a three-sided separately roofed bay

of french doors. Fanlit french doors open on to the verandah, and there are no windows. Like so many Queensland country houses there is no front hall or door, and entry is straight into the principal room, the dining room, which runs across the house from the front to the back, broken by an arch at its third point. The dining room occupies two bays of the elevation to the right of centre. On its right is the single-bayed drawing room and behind it the breakfast room. On the other side are four bedrooms reached via each other or through the verandah. The rooms are lined, walls and ceilings, with wide beaded boards which are painted and there is fine robust waxed cedar joinery. Interestingly the fanlights above the internal four-panelled doors are in the form of two-panelled shutters, all of which can be opened for ventilation in summer.

The separately roofed, 3 metre wide verandah, heavy with wistaria, is low to the ground, and there is a balustrade of lattice entwined with vine between its simple posts. An unusual feature is that its lined ceiling has

the boards running perpendicular to the walls.

Behind, the house forms itself into a 'U' around an underground water-storage tank with kitchen offices balancing the station office. Here the verandahs are shallower, and the kitchen verandah is screened by lattice. There is a header tank and, beyond, a meat room. Edwardian additions consist of a gabled bedroom wing to the side and a more exotic lanterned schoolroom pavilion which, with a picket fence, makes the final enclosure to the rear courtyard.

One of the features of Franklyn Vale is its wonderful garden. A large teardrop carriage loop the full length of the bungalow fronts the house; there is a centre parterre; and outside the drive is edged with a shrubbery with glimpses through to the Liverpool Mountains beyond. Scattered in the garden are cast-iron garden seats and a sophisticated tennis pavilion which suggests the hand of the Queensland Edwardian architect, Robin Dods. Like all good country-house gardens in this part of the world, it is marked by bunya pines and there is also a huge bottle tree.

Franklyn Vale looks over a wonderful mid Victorian homestead garden centred on a large carriage oval the length of the house. On the right is a mature bottle tree and behind a windmill. Bunya pines are a feature of the garden.

The tennis pavilion is a sophisticated Edwardian timber structure worthy of the Brisbane architect Robin Dods. It is an important element in the Franklyn Vale garden.

Behind the house is a courtyard flanked on the left by the kitchen, water tank and meat room and on the right by the striking Edwardian schoolroom pavilion complete with an unusual timber chimney.

The deep verandahs are heavy in wistaria. An interesting detail is the ceiling boards running at right angles to the wall. Lattice at the end screens the verandah sleepout. The low-slung verandah is an important part of this Queensland house.

Yanga is an old-fashioned design for its time: the balanced elevation, double pitch hipped roof and verandah valance are all details of the late Georgian period.

A much more consciously colonial house is **Yanga**, on the Murrumbidgee River in the Riverina area of New South Wales, built *c.* 1870 for Sir Charles Nicholson, Bt., who had acquired this vast station in 1866. Like Franklyn Vale the house was built for a manager, and Nicholson, a respected member of the colonial establishment, had by now returned to England and was living in a country house in Hertfordshire. Nicholson was a wealthy doctor who had been involved with almost all the cultural institutions of New South Wales including the founding of the University of Sydney. While he controlled vast pastoral interests he had always lived in Sydney.

Yanga is a bungalow which, in almost every way, follows the house design of the 1830s and 1840s. A double-pile plan with a hollow roof, it is seven bays across. The main door is fanlit with sidelights and is balanced by french doors. Inside there is a central hall broken by a broad archway, balanced on each side by two rooms, and beyond this again on each side are single-bayed end rooms which can only be reached from the verandah. This is encircled by a wide, separately roofed verandah supported by timber posts with a pretty valance. The house is sited on a rise and looks out to the east over its formal terraced garden to Lake Yanga. Here the garden is dominated not by the bunya pine, but by the jacaranda tree. The jacaranda is not a native species but had been imported from Brazil in the middle years of the century. The extraordinary thing about this ostensibly colonial Georgian bungalow is its construction. Each aperture is formed by adzed posts and between are drop log panels held to the posts by cleat. The logs of Murray pine still maintain their bark, as do the posts that support the verandah. Only the adzed frame and dressed timbers are painted, and this gives the house a particularly rustic quality. Again one suspects the same picturesque educated values we saw at Gracemere. It is a gentleman's rustic cottage in the wilderness.

Behind and to the side is the kitchen block with offices and quarters. Here the construction is similar, although some of the drop logs are adzed. This building suggests it could be earlier than the main house.

The house is built on the tip of a peninsula jutting into the lake, and on the road leading out to the house are the station buildings which make up the complex.

Yanga is the archetypal country house and represents the Georgian survival as distinct from a revival of colonial architecture. The symmetrical colonial bungalow was still alive.

Not only is the concept old-fashioned, so too is the detail. The elliptical fanlight and margined sidelights are typical 1840s features.

Yanga has an almost deliberately rustic construction. The horizontal pine logs still have their bark on, as do the verandah posts.

The back verandah of Yanga. Only the adzed uprights, the verandah valance and the joinery are painted, giving a striking effect. Wire birdproofs the ceiling.

A delightful and intact formal Victorian homestead garden is before the house on the east running down to Lake Yanga.

Aloes, a common feature of many Victorian gardens, edge the drive at Eeyeuk.

A more up to date although very restrained house is **Eeyeuk** west of Geelong in Victoria. This house was built for Alexander Dennis in 1874–75 on land his Cornish father, a successful pastoralist, had acquired in 1867. The architect for the house was Alexander Hamilton, and it is said to be his first building. (Hamilton is best remembered for his later country mansion, Talindert, built in 1889–91.) Eeyeuk is in effect a Victorian Italianate villa; unlike the similarly conservative Perricoota it has two fronts at right angles and is meant to be seen from the angle, with the domestic wing at the side behind. This wing was originally one-storeyed, but a second floor was added in 1902.

The picturesque idea is strengthened by the contemporary garden laid out by the architect. The drive comes in from the side in a way that the two fronts can be seen. In front of the main door the drive swells into a broad apron, and opposite is a delightful pleasure garden laid out in symmetrical looped paths edged with box hedging and which contained a rusticated summerhouse. The house in essence is three bays wide by two bays deep, but by bringing forward the rooms to the left of the central hall the basic box is broken into a picturesque composition. A more elaborate house would have had a tower at the internal corner, but Eeyeuk is not a house for show and represents the attitudes of a successful but conservative Wesleyan family.

This Italianate house is well built of local basalt, with an encircling concave-roofed verandah with cast-iron structure. The walls are relieved by quoins, and the boxed eaves to the

hipped roofs are bracketed. Inside the central hall is balanced at the front by the principal rooms, but the breakforward of the left-hand bay allows the stair to run across the house behind the dining room, with access under it to the verandah which provides a covered link to the attached kitchens and domestic offices. Probably the most interesting room is the ground-floor office which has its walls lined with prints cut from magazines. Such rooms have been popular since the eighteenth century, and notable examples are at Castletown in Ireland and at The Vyne in Hampshire, but in Australia such a room is a rarity. It was originally the school-room, and the decoration was done by the children of the house.

Right *The main front of Eeyeuk seen across the apron of lawn before the house. On the left is the service wing which had a first floor added in Edwardian times.*

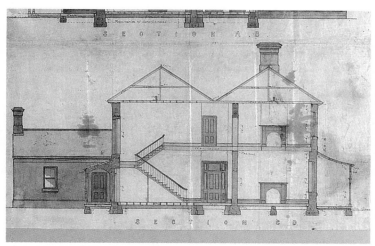

The cross-section of the architect's working drawing shows the staircase and the kitchen wing in its original single-storey form.

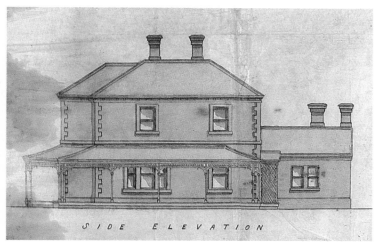

The side elevation of the working drawing shows a latticed porch over the door at the back of the hall and more of the original service wing.

The unusual name of this house is taken from the calls made by local yellowtail black cockatoos.

Left *A detail of the front corner of the house shows how closely the plan has been followed and how well it is built in local basalt.*

Opposite page *The old schoolroom at the back of the house has its walls lined with cuttings in the manner of eighteenth-century print rooms. The chimneypiece, wallpaper frieze and oak wallpaper dado are Edwardian c.1905.*

A much grander country house is **The Gums** in the Western District of Victoria built in 1876–77 for William Ross. Ross, a native of Inverness and a well-educated man, had been a very successful squatter on the Murray River. He bought The Gums in 1864, and there set about creating an estate that would illustrate his family's success in the new world and in which he could live the life of a Victorian country gentleman.

The house is in essence a symmetrical Italianate *palazzo* not dissimilar from the designs Leonard Terry had been using for bank buildings in the previous decade and which in 1858 he had used for the prestigious Melbourne Club. It is a very restrained design for the 1870s but one with respectable, almost aristocratic credentials.

The house is grand in scale, not dissimilar to Mona Vale but not as big. It is a completely symmetrical double-pile plan seven bays wide. The back pile is longer and oversails at the sides to provide broken bayed return elevations. It is a house with three fronts and in this respect is not dissimilar to such late Georgian designs as Killymoon. At the back the single-storeyed domestic quarters form a courtyard around a central underground water-storage tank. The house was obviously expensive, and the well-known Melbourne architect Joseph Reed (1823–90), whose design it was, was criticised for the expense. It cost in excess of £6000. However, the walls are not faced with stone but are

This Italian palazzo design is the work of the prominent Melbourne architect, Joseph Reed. The Gums is set in a fine Victorian garden focused on a large carriage oval.

The Gums is not a freestone house but stuccoed in grey Portland cement to simulate fine ashlar. The verandah detail is wood, domesticating the palazzo concept.

The long symmetrical front of the house seen in perspective under the branches of the sequoia or Wellingtonia, named after the great Duke of Wellington.

mocked up in imitation using Portland cement, a material that became increasingly popular with Victorian builders. Ross was not the sort of man to get himself into financial difficulties like Alfred Joyce at Norwood.

The handsome facades are well detailed with elaborate architraves to the large sash windows and rich modillions under the eaves of the hipped slated roofs. Before the door is a richly detailed pedimented Italianate porch flanked by encircling verandahs of timber construction which domesticate the *palazzo* idea. Before the house is a large oval carriage circle the length of the house, and beyond, encircling it in a semi-circle, is a shrubbery edged on the outer side by a hedged walk.

Inside the front hall is balanced by the dining room on the right and the drawing room on the left, each of which take up three bays of the facade, and the plan breaks down into smaller rooms behind. Ahead is an imperial staircase which forms a breakfront in the back wall of the house and is lit by a tall arched sash window. The whole is late Georgian in concept but up-to-date Italianate in detail, with quality plasterwork and marble chimneypieces in the principal rooms.

Contrasting to the stuccoed main block, the single-storeyed service wing is built of quarry-faced basalt. In the centre of the gravelled yard is an underground tank.

Above left Mature cedrus and pinus, common trees in a Victorian garden, stand beside the hedged walk which borders the pleasure garden before the house.

Left The main entrance is marked by a heavily detailed porch. Tall plate glass sash windows light the principal rooms.

This watercolour, done shortly after the completion of the house in 1877, shows how stark it looked before the garden developed.

Right Driza-Bone raincoats and Akubra hats, common apparel of Australian country life, help fill the coat room at the back of the house.

The imperial staircase at the back of The Gums is lit by a tall etched sash window with coloured margins typical of the period.

The study at the side of the house retains its ornate Italianate timber chimneypiece and gilt chimney glass.

The handsome dining room retains its original Victorian furniture and black marble chimneypiece purchased in Melbourne in 1876.

The side of the house looks out over a gravelled turning circle. The principal entrance is marked by a columned porch.

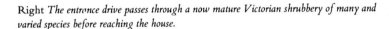

Mansfield Brothers' elegant villa design seen from within the mature Victorian garden of Burrungurroolong.

Right *The entrance drive passes through a now mature Victorian shrubbery of many and varied species before reaching the house.*

A similarly sized house which made much more of the architectural advances of the previous decades is **Burrungurroolong** outside Goulburn, built in 1880–81 for the rich pastoralist Andrew Gibson on land his father, Dr Andrew Gibson, had taken up in the late 1830s. The architect was George Allen Mansfield, who was as prominent in Sydney as Joseph Reed was in Melbourne. Both headed considerable architectural practices, designing everything from country houses to banks, public buildings and churches, and both played a prominent part in the establishment of professional Institutes of Architects in their respective states. Mansfield certainly acquainted himself with architectural theory, and various pattern books, like Calvert Vaux's *Villas and Cottages,* E. L. Tarbuck's *Builder's Practical Director* and Robert Kerr's *The Gentleman's House* can be seen as influencing his considerable output. Burrungurroolong is the sort of house that would have been inspired by Kerr, and although we might call it a mansion, in the parlance of the time it was to Mansfield simply a 'Villa Residence including Stable Offices'. It cost £5270.

The house is approached through open country and is set in a densely wooded garden of gardenesque design which runs down to the picturesque Mulwaree Chain of Ponds. This Italianate villa has three principal fronts, each different. The centre front is first seen after entering the pleasure garden and passing through the shrubbery. The drive swells out into a large circle to the right before the entrance porch. Across the garden stands the stable block, which is Gothic in style.

The picturesque composition in the house's exterior is reflected in the internal planning. Across the five-bay principal front is first the drawing room with its own three-sided bay breaking into the verandah, which here uses that wonderful invention, Portland cement, for its pavement. Then comes the dining room at right angles, with its long side looking out to the side. The balance of the front rectangle is taken up by the entrance hall, and behind this in the second pile is the staircase with handsome tripartite windows looking out into the rear service yard. The stair is balanced by the library beside the front door and breakfast room and servants' stair behind the dining room. Under the staircase, where a door leads into the central service courtyard, is a men's cloakroom complete with wash basin and W.C. – something that was increasingly to be found adjacent to the entrance halls of houses. As Kerr wrote, 'they are provided for the use chiefly of gentlemen visitors who can always find their way to the Entrance Hall without trouble, if nowhere else'.

Behind this front double-pile block, the building runs back in two single-pile two-storey wings with two-storeyed verandahs facing each other across a service yard. Beyond the breakfast room are the pantry, servants' hall, kitchen and other offices with servants' bedrooms above. In the facing wing reached only from outside is the station office, with a second entrance convenient to the carriage circle; then there is a schoolroom; and above these two rooms is the billiard room reached by an external stair within the two-storeyed verandah. One suspects that this allowed the billiard room to be used for the nasty male habit of smoking. Although Prince Albert had made smoking respectable in the 1840s, it still required separate accommodation. One suspects the tower room in such houses as Rosedale was originally set aside for smoking as well as for viewing the country. The male domain of office, cloakroom, smoking and billiard rooms was more and more to become a feature of the large country house.

At the bottom of the yard the court is enclosed by a single-storeyed range for fruit storage, general storerooms, cellar and laundry; beyond this again is the drying green. Burrungurroolong has all the features of a well-planned mid Victorian country house.

The exterior of the house is rendered and painted, the verandah is supported on cast-iron columns, and all the Italianate decoration is run or moulded in cement. Above the bracketed eaves the hipped roofs were, before 1925, covered with split shingles. Inside the majority of the joinery is cedar and is polished. Originally in the drawing room the joinery was painted white, highlighted in gilt. Andrew Gibson and William Ross were both Scots, and their houses have a conservative establishment quality which befits the idea of a Victorian gentleman belonging to an established family. As Kerr put it in *The Gentleman's House*, 'taste among the superior orders is adverse to rich or sumptuous effects.'

Much more smart and sumptuous, and suggesting new money, is **Mintaro**, north of Melbourne, built in 1882 for Captain Robert Gardiner to the design of architect James Gall. Gardiner began his adventurous life by running away to sea when he was sixteen on a South Seas whaling ship. Eventually he made his fortune running cargo ships.

The design suggests Gardiner wanted something to emulate Melbourne's Italianate Government House built during the previous decade, inspired by Osborne which Queen Victoria and Prince Albert had built on the Isle of Wight. It was a common idea for Victorian splendour.

Mintaro is a villa with three fronts, and its basic plan form is not dissimilar from Burrungurroolong, but on a smaller scale. The main block is a double pile, the front pile having an encircling two-storeyed parapeted arcade; and the back pile, oversailing to include the arcade, is astylar with boxed eaves. On the entrance front the last bay of the arcade, which is masked by the entrance porch, is taken up in a tall three-storeyed tower with a belvedere like Government House. Inside, the two principal rooms are at right angles, the residual area of the rectangle being the front hall. The back pile has the staircase which forms a breakfront in the back wall, flanked by two further rooms. This makes the main block into virtually a square on plan. Behind to the left is the two-storeyed servants' wing which is smaller in scale.

Despite its apparent splendour it is all a bit thin. The arcade has a cardboard quality, and the rendered decoration seems not as convincing as we have seen elsewhere. Inside, however, is splendid. The front hall, which with the staircase forms an 'L' on plan, is separated into three bays by lintels supported by plaster Corinthian columns and pilasters, and all the plasterwork and joinery is either marbled, wood-grained, gilded, stencilled or hand-painted. The surbase is cunningly painted in *trompe-l'oeil* and is not three-dimensional at all. The floor is richly finished with encaustic tiles. In the adjoining drawing room the ceil-

The generous entrance hall is distinguished by a fine cedar staircase and elaborately painted glass. The door under the stair leads to a water closet.

The drawing room is centred on a bay window which breaks the main garden front of the house. Edwardian photographs show that the joinery was originally painted white and highlighted with gilding.

Right *The high Victorian Gothic style of the stables contrasts with the Italianate style of the house. The building has been altered to accommodate motor cars.*

ing has hand-painted panels. As if to advertise the owner's parvenu status, these record the various facets of Captain Gardiner's career including his time as a whaler. Upstairs the bedrooms retain their original wallpapers, beautifully matched schemes of grasses and flowers, through the dado, surbase, filler and frieze.

By the 1880s Australian architecture was being affected by the Arts and Crafts movement in England, whose greatest single influ-

ence since the 1860s was that of William Morris. This in essence was a revival of medieval practices in craftsmanship and was strongly opposed to the 'machine'. It led to more naturalistic design and more honest use of materials. The so-called aesthetic movement which resulted from it was to influence the Australian house in the late Victorian period. There were also technical advances which made houses more comfortable.

Far left *Mintaro is a mid Victorian wedding cake design and undoubtedly took its cue from Melbourne's Government House built in the previous decade. The belvedere tower was a common feature of Victorian Italianate houses such as this.*

Left *The handsomely detailed arcades which encircle the front of the house are thin in section, with a cardboard quality.*

Left *The main garden front of the house looks out over the remains of a Victorian garden.*

The ceiling is painted on paper, the columns are scagliola, the walls are stencilled and the joinery is grained to simulate English oak.

Left *The elaborately detailed front hall is a crescendo of Victorian surface decoration. Every surface is finished to the highest standard and the floor is richly paved with English encaustic tiles.*

Late Victorian

The idea of a symmetrical verandahed house which had been built from the earliest years of Australian settlement was strongly established as the sort of house to build in the country. It can really be called the 'Georgian Survival', and a house like **Wiridgil** in the Western District of Victoria, although clothed in late Victorian dress, is really conceptually late Georgian. It was built in 1885, the architect being Albert Purchas, who had an established domestic and commercial practice. He had earlier (in 1857) designed Glenara which is a much more up to date country house for its time.

Interestingly Wiridgil was built by a rich 22-year-old bachelor. Thomas Manifold's family had been in Victoria since the 1830s, they were in *Burke's Colonial Gentry*, and he had been educated at Cambridge, was well travelled and was an up to date member of the Establishment. His house was not therefore necessarily meant to be conservative nor to impress anyone; it was part of the Australian ethos to build such a house in the 1880s, and rather like the Heidelberg school of painting it was Australian. The design owes nothing to American or English architectural thinking. It

Above *The low-spreading lines exemplified in Wiridgil, built in 1885, had by the late Victorian period become an Australian tradition. The pavilion in the left return of the verandah is a sympathetic Edwardian addition carried out for Edward Manifold who succeeded his brother at the house in 1895.*

Far left *The extensive garden is carried into the surrounding countryside by numerous plantings which form a park-like setting for the house.*

Left *The house is well built of local basalt, the body of the wall laid in squared random rubble. The bay windows balancing the front door carry through and break the roof line of the main front.*

The basalt walls of the house are shielded at the front with a cast-iron verandah heavy in wistaria.

Above right The use of contrasting materials to make polychromy was a late Victorian feature. At Wiridgil, the Italianate detailing is picked out in render against the more usual grey basalt or bluestone of the Western District.

Below The billiard room ceiling and joinery are respectively art nouveau and Maori in character, strong style influences of the late Victorian period.

Below right The focus of the male domain in the late Victorian house was the billiard room. Here the room is the result of Guyon Purchas' alterations for Edward Manifold.

Bottom right By the late Victorian period fitted bathrooms had become standard in large houses and even fitted handbasins had begun to appear. Here the bath and basin are set in polished cedar and St Anne's marble.

was an Australian house for an Australian country gentleman.

The main double-pile block stands forward of the rest of the house with balancing three-sided bays breaking into the verandah on either side of the front door. The tile-floored cast-iron-framed and separately roofed verandah is broken by a pediment, which breaks forward in the centre above the door. Set back behind the main block are separate balancing pavilions. The pavilion on the left contains the billiard room and study and that on the right the bedrooms. The house is built of grey basalt beautifully put together, with a corrugated-iron roof and all the up to date Italianate details we have seen in other houses.

Thomas Manifold died as a result of a hunting accident in 1895 and was succeeded by his brother, Edward, who was married. The

house was further aggrandised with various alterations, which included the construction of the dining room, and, by taking in the front hall and cross passage with the original dining room beside the front door, an impressive living hall which measured 10.5 × 9 metres was created. Because conceptually such a house was old-fashioned it did not mean it lacked all the up to date appurtenances associated with late Victorian country-house life. It had the male domain of study and billiard room, it had bathrooms close to the bedrooms (there were three in all), and its interiors were decorated in a way that owed a great deal to the English Arts and Crafts movement. The long main front of the house, covering eight rooms in total, looks out over a gravel apron and broad lawn edged with a semi-circular ha-ha wall (or sunken fence) to distant parkland.

Right *The dining room at the side of the house is one of the impressive Edwardian interiors formed by Guyon Purchas. There is an embayed window and fireplace set in an inglenook with columned archways which are intriguingly art nouveau.*

Opposite page *Guyon Purchas carried out numerous alterations during the early years of this century. The original dining room, front hall and cross hall were thrown into one to form an impressive living hall, a feature beloved of late Victorian and Edwardian architects.*

The picturesque roofscape of Alton seen from the forest. The dominant roof is that of the great hall and to the left is the lantern of the billiard room added later.

From virtually the start of colonisation, rich merchants, bankers and professional men had chosen to build houses outside the town, and early Sydney, Hobart and Adelaide were surrounded, at a distance, with villas in their own grounds, pleasure garden, kitchen garden, horse paddock and so on. Summerholme outside Hobart is one such house. But with the coming of the railways it became possible for rich city gentlemen to think of having country houses more than a carriage drive away. Encouraged by the idea of escaping the summer heat, hill stations were built in the Mount Lofty Ranges of South Australia, at Mount Wilson in New South Wales, Toowoomba in Queensland, and in Victoria at Mount Macedon and the Dandenong Ranges near Melbourne. Here people could not only recover their health but also indulge in English-style gardening.

The Australian manager of the English, Scottish and Australian Chartered Bank, Sir George Verdon, chose Mount Macedon to build his country house. Verdon was a well-educated and successful Victorian gentleman. He had been an M.P., treasurer of Victoria and the state's first agent-general in London. He was involved with most of the educational and artistic institutions of his day and was a friend of the English architect Pugin and of

William Wardell (1823–99) who designed the magnificent Gothic revival headquarters of the E.S. & A. Bank in Melbourne, built under Verdon's patronage in 1883–87. It is not surprising that a connoisseur like Verdon would want an artistic up to date design for his summer house.

Alton is near the top of Mount Macedon and is approached up a steep and sharply bending country lane, submerged in the forest; the drive brings you to the side of the house. Before the house is a series of banked terraces running down the steep slope, with a tennis court reached by stairs. Paths wind between conifers, maples, rhododendrons and azaleas.

The house is suitably picturesque for its setting, with tall gables and dormer windows. It is timber framed on a brick foundation, and both the roofs and walls above sill level are tile hung. The roofs are perversely picturesque: some are gabled, some jerkin headed and some mansarded. Its appearance is partly due to its construction. Starting as a small three-bayed cottage in 1874, it grew with the major addition (to the left) of a great hall and bedroom wing by 1882. Later a billiard room and library were added behind.

Inside is dominated by the wonderful great hall/living room, a feature beloved of late Victorian architects. The walls of the principal rooms are lined vertically with polished V-jointed New Zealand kauri, and the ceilings are finished in alternating diagonally boarded panels. The dados, doors and chimneypieces are richly detailed in Tasmanian blackwood and exotic New Zealand timbers in Gothic design – very much in the style made popular by the English architect Charles Eastlake in his *Hints on Household Taste* published in 1872.

The front of the house looks down a series of banked terraces to a tennis court. The verandahed section of the house dates from 1874. To the left are the great hall and bedroom wing built in the early 1880s.

One is tempted to think the transformation from cottage to house was carried out by an English architect such as Norman Shaw, but the finish of the interior makes it unlike any English house and one suspects the influence is American from the contemporary shingle-hung houses of New England. It is certainly a very advanced design for Australia at the time. Although Verdon is said to have designed it himself, it is most probably the work of William Wardell. Some of the details, for example, are quite similar to those in the Manager's flat (where Verdon lived in Melbourne) at the top of the contemporary E.S. & A. Bank. In its way the interiors of this fine Arts and Crafts house are as unique as Queensland houses such as Gracemere.

The house from the rear. The walls are hung with English terracotta tiles by Burton & Sons of Staffordshire.

Left *The dining room within the original 1874 cottage. The interior is lined with kauri with more exotic New Zealand timbers used for panelling and fittings. The portrait at the end of the room is of George Nicholas who purchased the property in 1929.*

Right *The side of the great hall. In the bay window is leadlight by Belhams of London. Asbestos shingles replace the original terracotta on the roof.*

Opposite page *The great hall is the principal room of the house. The walls are lined with New Zealand kauri and the wainscot is of Tasmanian blackwood with panels of New Zealand totara. The elaborate wooden chimneypiece bears the arms of Sir James Verdon who claimed connexion with the Earls of Shrewsbury of Alton Towers in Staffordshire.*

Over *The low-spreading lines of Meningoort are in part the result of rebuilding on a site where a house had stood since 1852. The strong geometry of the layout makes one of the boldest garden designs in Victoria.*

Meningoort in the Western District of Victoria is a very different sort of house of the 1880s. The house as we see it today was completed in 1887 designed by Charles D'Ebro, who interestingly designed Stonnington, the Melbourne house of John Wagner (joint principal of Cobb & Co. and partner with Alexander Robertson in Perricoota). His work is usually more stylistic. Peter McArthur had held the property since 1840, and the first house, a symmetrical double-pile verandahed bungalow built in 1852, stood on the same site as the present main front of the house.

One of the features of the house is its siting which is formed into one of the boldest pieces of garden design in Victoria. It is dramatically positioned on a man-made terrace below Mount Meningoort, and the axis of the house and the mountain top is aligned with Mount Leura 16 kilometres away down a long avenue of blue gums. This is the principal drive to the house. It ends in a carriage circle and is set below the terrace, and the house is reached by axial flights of steps first to the terrace and then to the verandah. Terraces extend into the richly planted park-like landscape on either side. Such a strong setting undoubtedly discouraged building anywhere else, and the old house was added to. First an Italianate pavilion was added to the north, then a balancing pavilion was added to the south. This was achieved by 1885. Then in 1886–87 the 1850s house was taken down and replaced by the present main front.

The composition is not dissimilar to Wiridgil, but the spreading verandah form is

much less excitingly developed, which probably results from the strong restraints of the site and the order in which the complex was constructed. Also the Scottish-born Peter McArthur had been living at Meningoort for forty-six years, he was sixty-six, and even though he had remarried in 1886 he obviously preferred the traditions of the place to anything modern or pretentious. He was one of the most established pastoralists in Victoria.

Inside the house is similarly conservative, and the decoration (much of which survives) belongs very much to the mid Victorian period. It is another example of Georgian survival but for reasons quite different to Wiridgil.

The fact that the main front is asymmetrical is not readily apparent. The bay window which breaks into the verandah is not picked up in the roof line.

Below left *The library retains its 1880s decoration. The ceiling is stencilled, there is a wallpaper frieze above the picture rod, and there is a body and dado wallpaper.*

Below *The drawing room retains its original painted ceiling decoration and white marble chimneypiece. The furnishing reflects the interwar Georgian revival taste.*

The late Victorian billiard room was commonly housed in a separate pavilion with a roof lantern for natural lighting and for ventilation for the cigarette smoking which was meant to be carried out in such places.

The picturesque main garden front of Forest Lodge looks out over a croquet lawn and turns its back on the approach to the house. The crenellations and tall chimneys are rendered details to the otherwise stone house.

The entrance is via a Gothic porch which breaks into the verandah. The door is detailed in high Victorian manner with diagonal boarding in stop chamfered framing.

Left John Bagot was succeeded at Forest Lodge in 1910 by his son Walter, an eminent architect, who carried out extensive alterations to the garden. His devotion to Italy is illustrated by this Medici vase purchased there.

In 1890 Ernest Bayer (1852–1908) designed a more advanced house in the Mount Lofty Ranges as a summer residence for John Bagot, the grandson of Captain Charles Bagot who had settled in South Australia in 1840 and become a rich pastoralist and mine owner. John Bagot no doubt wanted a house that was as traditional as it was smart. The governor of South Australia had built a country house in the ranges at Marble Hill in 1879, and its Gothic style set the tone.

Forest Lodge is not nearly as avant-garde as Alton, but its picturesque design is equally suited to its romantic site. Situated at the end of a long drive in a beautiful mountain garden, unlike other villas it is not approached at the angle to show its two principal fronts but from the back of the house, from one side. The entrance front is seen first, then the drive passes the front door to a turning circle, which allows, on the return, a glimpse of the garden front of the house which faces a terraced croquet lawn. Forest Lodge is a Gothic-style villa with two fronts at right angles. The design is complex. There are three principal rooms on the ground floor. The bow-ended drawing room to the right of the front door is balanced by the smoke room, and behind is the dining room separated by a cross hall. Unlike almost all the other houses of this style the tower is not over the front door, but behind, in the angle formed by the dining and drawing rooms at the end of the cross hall;

under it is the principal staircase. The entrance is marked by a Gothic porch with a room above. At the side two domestic wings extend out to form a service yard.

Forest Lodge is built of warm sandstone quarried on the property, and the oversailing roof is sheeted in corrugated iron. A verandah of cast-iron construction (G. E. Fulton & Co., Adelaide) over a tiled terrace balances the porch and wraps around the base of the tower and dining room on the garden front of the house. The tower apertures, the bow and the main entrance are marked with Gothic label moulds. The crenellations to the tower and the tall barley-twist Gothic chimneys are in fact worked up in cement. The walls are broken by tall casement windows, set singly or in pairs. The design is somehow American, and one is reminded of the designs published by Calvert Vaux.

Inside the hall is suitably dark; it retains its aesthetic-taste wallpaper and high dado of analyptic wallpaper (embossed wallcovering). Combined with dark oak grained joinery and high-quality leadlights which include the Bagot arms, it makes for a most successful late Victorian interior. John Bagot was succeeded at Forest Lodge by his son Walter Bagot (1880–1963) who was a distinguished Adelaide architect, much interested in Italian Renaissance architecture. He further aggrandised the garden to make it probably the most successful formal landscape in Australia. The main rooms were redecorated by him, and in 1921 he added a second storey to the service wing to left of the entrance front. Like all good work it is indiscernable.

In Queensland by the late Victorian period a particular form of timber construction was being used almost universally in the north of the country to create a character of building that is uniquely Australian. At the beginning of the nineteenth century the idea of a stud frame wall – i.e. 100 × 50 mm vertical studs at 450 mm set into a bottom plate and supporting a top plate – was well known and much used in England, particularly in the south-east of the country. It was the form of construction used for lesser buildings and was used in grand buildings for internal partitions. When used for farmhouses the studs were usually filled in between with brickwork or some other material, as insulation, and usually but not always sheeted externally with feather-edged weatherboards. It was a simple quick form of construction, and in a country like Australia, particularly on the east coast where timber was plentiful, it was much used by early settlers. The 1818 section of Woolmers in Tasmania is an example of this. So too is The Springs in western New South Wales, although there in a much warmer climate no brick nogging was used and the house was lined inside with horizontal boarding as well. In the hot north even this form of construction was found to be too hot, and from about the 1860s the external lining was omitted, showing the stud framing as a skeleton. This type of construction was used in other hot climates such as the Caribbean.

Left *The fine mountain garden at Forest Lodge is in fact an arboretum of exotic trees to provide endless shady walks.*

Below *The entrance front of the house seen from the turning circle. The upper storey at the rear is a sympathetic addition to one of the service wings added by Walter Bagot.*

Bottom *Wyaralong homestead is seen across the parched summer landscape of south-eastern Queensland.*

Wyaralong in south-eastern Queensland is an example of this type of country house. Set high off the ground – which is another characteristic of the northern house – the house is on stumps, its semi-basement filled in by a diagonally formed trellis of sawn timber. Above, everything is dressed and painted and the house is ostensibly a verandahed bungalow with separately convex-roofed verandah. There is a pretty valance, richly detailed verandah posts and a nice dowelled balustrade with pretty gates at the top of each timber staircase which descends into the garden. There is a certain lightness about the house which makes it unlike any other house we

Left The setting of this typical Queensland house is marked by palms, hoop pines and jacaranda.

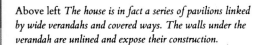

A bedroom pavilion was added at the side of the house c.1907. The late Victorian verandah detail of posts and balustrade is continued from the earlier house.

Above left The house is in fact a series of pavilions linked by wide verandahs and covered ways. The walls under the verandah are unlined and expose their construction.

The small front hall leads straight into the dining room which retains its Edwardian dining room furniture.

have seen in this book. But it is really in the shelter of the verandah that the house shows its true character. Unlike all the other timber houses we have seen, there is no external lining. In essence the house was originally a three-bayed double-pile pavilion, with a central fanlit half-glazed door balanced by fanlit french doors, which again characteristically of this region open outwards.

There is a narrow front hall, between two balancing rooms, leading behind into a large dining room with a bow into the side verandah and a shallow archway at its third point. This room has a fireplace, the only one in the house. Behind, reached across the verandah by a latticed covered way, are the detached kitchen and offices. The studwork is straight off the saw, and the internal lining behind is tongue-and-grooved, V-jointed vertical boards. The corner panels, i.e. between the french doors and external corners, are cross-braced like a St Andrew's Cross adding detail to the facade. The internal partitions are not studded, and the vertical boards stretch from floor to ceiling, stiffened by a horizontal dressed rail at midpoint in each wall panel.

The remarkable feature of the interior of the late Victorian Queensland house is its lack of detail. Except for the panelling in the doors the detail is as chaste as can be.

The rear view of the Edwardian bedroom pavilion has characteristics which relate it to the early twentieth century colonial revival.

Obviously, the builders had to decide which way the wall was to be faced, and at Wyaralong the rails are in the front hall and along the inner wall of the dining room.

The house would appear to have been added to soon after its construction by a further bay of rooms on the north. This section of the house was built by Campbell MacDonald. In 1906 the property was purchased by Colin Philp, the eldest son of Sir Robert Philp who in 1863 with Sir James Burns had formed the well-known shipping firm of Burns Philp & Co.

In *c*.1907 the Philps added yet another bed-room pavilion to the north, joined by open verandahs. This symmetrically composed building around a central chimney has wide verandahs filled in with corner weather-boarded box rooms at the back to make the western verandah *in antis*. This building is more sophisticated in form and reflects a refinement in construction which became common in Edwardian Queensland. Here the external walls are treated like the internal partitions of the earlier house. They are protected by the verandah, and the stiffening rails are moulded, and the vertical boards (now narrower) are V-jointed. The bungalow roof covers the deep verandah as well, the rafters carried down over the verandah plate and lined on the underside with the same V-jointed boards. This contrasts to the earlier verandah which has no framing at all, the convex iron reaching from wall to verandah plate. In all there are about 20 rooms and offices, all linked by verandahs and covered ways entwined with bougainvillea.

Wyaralong is still painted eau-de-Nil, Brunswick green and white outside, and its simple, painted and unadorned interiors make it a sharp contrast to the heavily detailed and richly decorated interiors of the south.

A typical, almost archetypal late Victorian country house of the south is **Talindert** in the Western District of Victoria, built in 1889–91 for the Hon. James Chester Manifold and designed by Alexander Hamilton, whose first design was Eeyeuk (see the previous chapter) built in 1875. It is that same old-fashioned survival we saw at Meningoort: the house of a well-established pastoral family. Although here not restricted by an earlier house and landscape, it dissolves into much the same solution. The house is approached through open parkland, and the drive sweeps around on to the axis of the house and up in a straight

Like Meningoort, Talindert sits at the centre of a very structured landscape. This archetypal two-storeyed late Victorian house was designed by Alexander Hamilton.

run to a turning circle before the door. The approach is flanked by shrubbery set well back. It is really quite eighteenth century in feeling, something that has no doubt been

strengthened by Georgian revival taste of the twentieth century. There are vistas to the countryside and to the orchard and the kitchen garden behind the house.

Talindert makes nothing of the picturesque, it is not a villa, it is meant to be seen straight on. In effect it has only one front; two-storeyed, rendered in grey Portland cement, moulded into Italianate detail, the main three-bay-wide double-pile block breaks forward of a larger back section, which contains on the right-hand side the billiard room. There are further Edwardian additions at the back designed by Guyon Purchas in 1907. The front section is encircled on its three sides by a two-storeyed verandah of cast-iron construction. Before the door this breaks forward, picking up the breakfront in the wall of the house. Under the balancing verandah, three-sided bows break into the tiled-floored verandah beside the front door.

Inside, the plan form is no different from a late Georgian archetypal house like Wickford in Tasmania; the central hall balanced on either side by two rooms with the staircase at the back behind an arch which at Talindert is of course more elaborate and late Victorian in character. It is not just the

Portland cement allowed all sorts of elaborate stone detailing to be cheaply copied. Dentils, architraves, mouldings, even vermiculated stones have been imitated in cement.

Top left *From the first floor balcony one gets an impression of how the countryside has been organised into a park setting of considerable quality.*

Above left *Within the verandah, bay windows break forward from the principal rooms beside the front door. The walls are rendered in grey Portland cement.*

Left *Skilful imitation was the order of the day in the Victorian period. Here a door has been grained in imitation of English oak. The door retains its original crystal doorknob and porcelain key escutcheon.*

The late Victorian billiard room at the side of the house retains its plasterwork, picture rail and joinery. The six-panelled door reflects the revived interest in eighteenth-century taste. The chimneypiece is Edwardian and over it hangs a portrait of Sir Chester Manifold who succeeded his father in 1942 and to whose period the decoration belongs.

The richly detailed stair hall has lost its surface decoration but its fine joinery and sumptuous late Victorian plasterwork are intact.

masculine detail, it is also the scale that marks it as late Victorian. Typical of the Victorian country house there is the important male domain of the study and billiard room.

James Manifold was imbued with the same values as his older brother Thomas, although Talindert is somehow not as successful and not as obviously Australian as the low-spreading Wiridgil built in the decade before.

More up to date is **Wairoa**, the summer residence of the mining magnate William Horn, built in South Australia's Mount Lofty Ranges in 1893. It is Queen Anne in style. From the 1870s, avant-garde and artistic English architects had begun to look at red-brick vernacular houses in the Home Counties (around London) – buildings often enriched by Flemish gables and details that mark the reign of Dutch William of Orange and Queen Mary at the end of the seventeenth century. This revival became known inexplicably as 'Queen Anne' and was very much a revival of eighteenth-century taste; also for the first time there was an appreciation of antique collecting in the form of seventeenth and eighteenth-century furniture and oriental rugs. This revival of English vernacular architecture is in contrast to earlier exotic revivals and is more parallel to and an extension of the Gothic revival. Its influence on Australia was quite unmarked until the 1880s, and it is really only in the 1890s that buildings began to appear which can be styled Queen Anne. Probably the first real example was Caerleon in Sydney designed by the English architect Maurice B. Adams and built in 1885 for Charles Fairfax of the newspaper family.

Wairoa is approached down a long drive entered by a lodge with elaborate wooden gates. Close to the house the drive skirts the contemporary pleasure garden on the left below the house and brings you to a turning circle before the house. The stables and kitchens are behind to the left.

While Wairoa is essentially Queen Anne, it has overtones that make it remarkably Australian. The walling is actually limestone rubble which so characterises South Australian architecture. This is trimmed with red bricks for quoins, arches, strings, window surrounds and chimneys. The house is particularly broken in form, with numerous gables breaking forward. One at the front corner breaks

forward at an angle of 45 degrees, which adds greatly to the idea of seeing the house from the approach drive. This use of the 45 degree bay was to be very much played up in the Edwardian period.

Elaborate bargeboards which trim the gables relate more to the carpenters' Gothic of New England in the United States than anything English. Between the gabled breakfronts are conventional late Victorian two-storeyed verandahs structured in cast iron which are typically Australian. The iron is by G. E. Fulton of Adelaide. It is that sort of hybrid design which was to develop in Australia into what is now known as Federation style.

To the right of the main block of the

house, linked by a crenellated brick archway, is a detached two-storey gabled wing, in fact the male domain.

Entry to the house is by a porch with a room above which breaks forward between the verandahs. Entry is made straight into a large hall at the front corner, with the staircase rising against the outer wall. There is a fireplace, and the hall has that living/hall quality of the fashionable English country house. To the left is the drawing room and behind it the dining room balanced across a hall with the morning room. Upstairs a cast-iron bridge behind the archway provides an external link to the bachelors' room, under which is the smoking room.

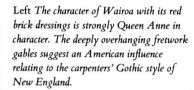

Left *The character of Wairoa with its red brick dressings is strongly Queen Anne in character. The deeply overhanging fretwork gables suggest an American influence relating to the carpenters' Gothic style of New England.*

Below left *Cast-iron steps are an intriguing detail for the main approach into the fine late Victorian garden laid out below the house by William Horn in 1893–96.*

Below *The fine cast-iron decoration of the verandahs is from the Adelaide foundry of G. E. Fulton.*

Far left *Surviving Morris curtains and wallpaper in the morning room. The wallpaper in this room is Pink and Rose, designed in c.1890.*

Left *The woven wool curtains in the dining room are the famous Peacock and Dragon pattern designed by Morris in 1878.*

Far left *The wallpaper in the bachelors' room in the male domain at the side of the house is the famous Willow Bough design of 1887.*

Left *The wallpaper that survives in a first floor bedroom is Lily, designed by Morris in 1873.*

Wairoa is an avant-garde design which looks forward to the next decade. Even more smart and trendsetting was its interior decoration. Although much use has been made of William Morris designs in fashionable modern restorations in Australia, it is true to say he was virtually unknown by nineteenth-century Australians; and although many papers and fabrics in the manner of Morris were used, nothing actually from Morris & Co. is known – with one prominent exception, the Barr Smith family, and their family connections, the O'Halloran Giles.

In 1896 Horn sold his new house complete with its garden preliminary to his 'going home' to live in a country house in England. The house was bought by the businessman and philanthropist Robert Barr Smith, who in 1863 had founded the pastoral firm Elder Smith & Co. with his brother-in-law Sir Thomas Elder. Barr Smith bought the property for his son Tom Barr Smith and daughter-in-law Mary as a country house.

Mr and Mrs Robert Barr Smith were devotees of Morris. They, their son Tom and their daughter Jean, who married Thomas O'Halloran Giles, furnished their houses in Adelaide and in the hills with furniture, carpets, papers and fabrics from Morris & Co. Tom Barr Smith even bought Hammersmith carpets for the Adelaide Club, to which he belonged. Surviving at Wairoa are various papers and fabrics: in the morning room, Pink and Rose wallpaper with Trent chintz; in the bachelors' room, Willow Bough wallpaper; and in the bedrooms, Lily wallpaper and Medway chintz. In the dining room there are Peacock and Dragon woven wool curtains. The Queen Anne taste and the Morris decoration make Wairoa a quite advanced ensemble. The family continued to occupy the house until 1965.

The great bungalow of the 'front house' at Wellington Lodge has very high ceilings and extremely wide, cast-iron verandahs.

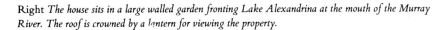

Right *The house sits in a large walled garden fronting Lake Alexandrina at the mouth of the Murray River. The roof is crowned by a lantern for viewing the property.*

On the broad featureless plains of the south-east of South Australia on 30 000 hectares (72 000 acres) taken up by the Scottish settler Allan McFarlane in 1843, his son Allan McFarlane junior, then in his sixties, built a very grand but conservative and typical late Victorian country house. The main house at **Wellington Lodge** is in essence a huge asymmetrical bungalow with ceilings 5.5 metres (18 feet) high and with wide verandahs roofed in convex iron supported by cast-iron columns with friezes and balustrades by Stewart & Harley's Sun foundry in Adelaide. Fanlit doors, as distinct from french doors, lead on to the verandah which is paved in cement, and the rubble limestone walls are similarly rendered in imitation of squared rubble with rusticated quoins and architraves. The hipped roof of corrugated iron is dominated by a viewing lantern to take in the vast property.

The old house still survives behind the 'front house', in its original form a typical verandahed bungalow of the late Georgian period built low with verandahs *in antis* and linked by verandahs to wings containing kitchens and offices.

It was here that the Duke of Edinburgh, the same royal prince we have seen at Mona Vale and Perricoota, stayed in 1867. The courtyards and open areas between the various pavilions have since been roofed, and the complex of spreading iron roofs is now like some extraordinary vast tent.

The reason for the siting of the house is Lake Alexandrina, the freshwater lake where the Murray River enters the sea and from which the property still draws its water. To protect the house from the wind and make it secure in this remote place on the open plains, the original McFarlane had a limestone wall 2.4 metres high built around the house, forming a large rectangle with one side open to the lake on the west. Within were the pleasure

The principal entrance is marked by a typical late Victorian front door. The balancing doors are half-glazed single doors. The walls and verandah floor are finished in grey Portland cement.

gardens and kitchen garden; outside against the walls were the workshops, storerooms and station offices, which formed a considerable village of structures at Wellington Lodge. A walled garden on this scale is rather like that found at English country houses.

Inside, the 'front house' is very conservative. A through hall is broken by an archway, behind which rises the stair to the lookout. On the right is the drawing room, which takes up the whole southern end of the building and looks out into the flower garden. From the stair hall a cross hall which has joinery still grained as oak leads to the bedrooms, and there is one bathroom (a second was added for the visit of the Duke and Duchess

of York in 1927). The dining room and study survive in the old house, and at the end behind everything else a billiard room was built on, reached from outside via a verandah.

Deep verandahs and large tent-like roofs were the tradition for the country house, and except in the south-east of Australia few gentlemen were dissuaded from building anything else – even a gentlemen of the calibre of Alfred Greenup. The son of a Cambridge-educated doctor from Parramatta, Alfred was also well educated, widely travelled and fluent in Greek. Indeed it is probably this sophistication that allowed him to synthesise the Australian vernacular idea of a house with what he had seen elsewhere.

A wide ogee shaped corrugated-iron roof spans from the walls of the house to the verandah plate.

Looking out across the garden of Wellington Lodge to Lake Alexandrina. The fine cast iron of the verandah columns is from Stewart and Harley's Sun foundry in Adelaide.

The complex from the rear. The original house is below the tower and on the left is the billiard room added at the time of the 'front house' which dominates the group.

The rubble limestone wall with its rendered coping and cast-iron cresting which encloses the court at the rear of the house.

The drawing room retains its late Victorian chimneypiece and plasterwork. The decoration relates to the visit of the Duke and Duchess of York in 1927.

Looking from the staircase below the tower to the front door. In the front hall is an English square piano, part of the furnishing of the house built in 1843.

Left *'Between the houses', a court built in what had been the verandah of the first house. This view is taken from the 'front house' and shows the front wall of the old house.*

Although ostensibly just another veran-dahed house, **Wylarah** is in fact very sophis-ticated in a particularly Australian way. The house, built in 1891 and designed by Greenup, is really a single pile of rooms built in a 'U'. The wide verandah carries around the outside and across the top of the U as a range of skillion rooms. The centre of the U is covered by a double gabled roof, with its rafters exposed under sarking boards and with glazed lighting in the southern gables. The house in effect is a symmetrical villa with its entrance front on the south and with the three other verandahed elevations looking out to the garden. It is a house to be seen in the round. The main north front is marked by a central flèche, which contains a bell, and the verandah has a balustrade of the St Andrew's Cross pattern. Only the sashes, doors and ver-andah woodwork are painted.

The house is entered via a porch *in antis* in the south wall straight into the central living

Wylarah is a single pile of rooms built in the form of a 'U' with an encircling verandah carried across its bottom as a skillion of rooms. The central space is roofed by two gables.

The house is a villa to be seen in the round. There are three verandahed elevations to the garden and here the entrance front with a central porch in antis. To the right is the detached bath house built of corrugated iron.

Below *The house is raised on stumps and between the posts is a verandah balustrade of the lightest construction. At Wylarah, only the sash doors and the square stop chamfered verandah posts and plate are painted.*

hall. It is, in Australian terms, equal to the 'great hall' revival of the late Victorian country house in England – a room for multipurpose use, part living room, part meeting place, a venue for games – a room that led the way to the open-plan house. All other rooms of the house open from this, the bedrooms, the dining room, the drawing room and even the kitchen. In the bedrooms are fitted wardrobes. Only the bathroom was detached on the west, lined with ripple iron. All the internal doors are half-glazed below

fanlights, and there are french doors leading on to the verandah.

Not only is the form of the house sophisticated, so too is the way its timbered walls are constructed. The walls of the skillion rooms have cypress pine boards laid horizontally, beaded to the exposed studwork. These and the other walls under the verandah and the internal partitions are unique. They are formed of vertical ironbark studs at 600 mm (2 feet) centres. Each bay is divided into three, and within each panel are fitted vertically

wide cypress pine boards beaded in by pine scotias to the ironbark. The walls are the same on each face. The ceilings are lined with 150 mm (6 inches) wide plain cypress boards. Again a comparison with panelled rooms of Tudor England cannot be overlooked. It is a house influenced by the Australian vernacular, the picturesque idea of a villa and the English Gothic revival. Yet it is nothing if not a uniquely Queensland building and perhaps a high point for domestic design in this country.

Left *The french doors are typical of the late Victorian period. Unusual for this region, they all originally opened inward, like a southern house.*

Below *The verandahs are quite magical at Wylarah. The sarking boards are beaded but otherwise the detail is unexpected.*

In the entrance porch hang the trappings of country life. In this section the cypress planks are placed horizontally and beaded to the studs. Both faces of the wall are the same.

Left *The dining room is typical of all the rooms in the house. The ironbark studs contrast with the cypress pine ceiling and panels held in place by hoop pine scotias. The sideboard and refectory table, conceived in an Arts and Crafts manner, were made for the house of native timbers.*

Below left *The main garden front of the house is symmetrical about a central bell flèche. The brick chimneys have moulded strings. The roof has always been constructed of corrugated iron.*

Below *The walls are of iron-bark studs, each bay broken by horizontal noggings. Within this frame are vertical planks of cypress pine tongued together and held by scotias of hoop pine.*

Above *The central living hall looking back towards the drawing room. All the internal doors are half-glazed.*

Top *Looking from the drawing room into the central living hall. The main front door is at the end and in the centre of the room is a refectory table of Tasmanian blackwood.*

In contrast to the very Australian country house of the late Victorian period was the house that could almost be in England. This house was found in those places where climatic considerations were not particularly important, as we have seen in hill stations or in the extreme south-east of the country. One such house is **Blackwood** in south-western Victoria built in 1891–92 for the rich pastoralist Robert Blackwood Ritchie and designed by the Melbourne architect Walter Butler (1864–1949). That it is such an English house, such an Arts and Crafts house, is not surprising as Butler had trained in England with J. D. Sedding (1838–91), a noted church restorer; he was a friend of William Lethaby (1857–1931), an influential figure in the Society for the Protection of Ancient Buildings; and he was accepted in the Arts and Crafts and domestic revival circles centred on William Morris (1834–96) and Norman Shaw (1831–1912). He ardently admired Norman Shaw, the most successful domestic architect of his day, and this is evidenced in the numerous houses he designed for wealthy businessmen and pastoralists in Victoria and New South Wales.

Like Shaw, Butler strove not so much to create a style but to create atmosphere, and Blackwood is a remarkable example of this. It is a new assembly of old elements, a cluster of roofs of different heights, stone mullioned windows and timber-framed ones, small windows and large ones, high rooms and low rooms, all skilfully mixed up together. There are Gothic arches, Tudor windows, seventeenth-century chimneystacks, half-timbering, tile hanging, basalt walls and stone walls, and inside there are inglenooks,

This view could be of an English house. The fact that it is single-storeyed and has a Marseille tiled roof are clues to its location. Blackwood was built in 1891–92 and designed by Melbourne architect Walter Butler.

Left The bay window is reminiscent of Queen Anne style windows in contemporary English buildings, particularly those of the architect Norman Shaw.

Below Cypresses and other pine trees crowd the hill on which the house sits. It is the concept of a revived Tudor manor house in the antipodes.

The dining room or hall is richly panelled in blackwood and features a fitted sideboard.

Above left The side elevation of the house reveals its true nature. It is a cluster of roofs of different heights and shapes. The verandah is linked to the drawing room and the mullioned window lights the dining hall.

Left At the corner of the drawing room is a raised corner turret with window seats. It provides a place to sit and view the countryside.

Opposite page The dining room resembles a baronial hall, with a massive chimneypiece, panelled dado and barrel-vaulted roof. It is almost Tudor in concept, part of the so-called Queen Anne revival. The room retains its original furniture and is hung with portraits of the family.

wainscotting, and changes in level. Seen on its hill surrounded by cypresses, Blackwood could well be an English manor house. It is quaint, it is 'Old English'. The thing that makes Blackwood Australian is that it is single-storeyed; it is indeed a vast bungalow. No English house like this would ever have been on one floor.

Entry is via the expected great hall, complete with impressive fireplace and high ceiling. To the left is the drawing room, and behind at right angles the dining room with open board lined roof and high wainscotting, all achieved in Tasmanian blackwood timber. The drawing room opens on to a verandah at the side and has the intriguing detail of a corner turret at mezzanine level reached by a stair and fitted with seats to provide a view of the countryside. Such bays are often found in English houses but usually only a step above the main room. To the right of the front main hall are the bedrooms.

This house represents the continued idea of gentlemen wanting to create another England in the great south land. The desire for this sort of house was to be further encouraged by the journal *Country Life* which each week after it first appeared in 1897 illustrated old English houses.

Not all pastoralists had the desire to build houses that could be English. As we have seen, the Australian idea of a country house was firmly established. One of the great Australian country houses of the late Victorian period is **Boree Cabonne** built in 1897 by Lancelot Smith, whose father, John Smith, had established his family on the central western plains of New South Wales in the late 1830s. In the 1840s he had acquired Boree Cabonne with numerous other runs. The first house at Boree Cabonne was a low verandahed bungalow of the late Georgian type, to which in the 1870s a red-brick 'bachelors' wing in the form of another verandahed bungalow was added. This wing survives beside the big house built on the site of the original.

In concept Boree Cabonne makes little of what advances had been made in architectural thought in the previous decades, except perhaps that it is not preoccupied with the late Georgian plan form which restricts such archetypal houses as Talindert. The house is in effect a large rectangle on plan, with another rectangle almost as large, at the back, on the left, built at right angles, for the domestic

offices and maids' quarters. This wing is no smaller in scale than the main wing, and all is encircled by deep two-storeyed verandahs. On the front of the house the columns and balustrade are cast iron. On the back the columns are timber. The off-centre entrance is marked by a red-brick porch built within the verandah at ground-floor level. The walls of the house are red brick with cement dressing, and the verandah is paved in cement.

There are four principal rooms on the ground floor – the two front rooms balancing the encaustic-tiled hall being at right angles to each other, billiard room on the right, drawing room with bowed end on the left. This bow is the only element that breaks the rectangular exterior. Behind the billiard room is the office, and behind the drawing room on the other side of the staircase, which breaks into the back verandah, is the dining room with access directly into the service wing. Interestingly the billiard room has moved up front and is now very much part of the house; the office behind and the adjoining lavatory reached outside from the verandah has brought the male domain into the centre of the house. The billiard room increasingly became the central feature of Edwardian country houses. It was another use for the living hall.

Upstairs the five bedrooms have fitted wardrobes, and the principal bedroom, over the drawing room, not only has its own dressing room but a fitted bath and shower as well. There is another bathroom with W.C. at the top of the stairs. Houses were slow to acquire internal bathrooms. Many had W.C.s from the 1830s, but bathing continued to be done in hipbaths until well into the mid Victorian period. An early fitted bath from c.1840 survives at Aberglassyn in New South Wales, and several survive from the 1870s, but it was not until the 1880s that they really became common and then there was usually only one for quite large houses.

The house is fitted with cedar joinery, and all doors have opening fanlights to allow for cross-ventilation. The broad verandah is reached downstairs only by the hall and office doors, while upstairs every room has french doors opening on to the verandah.

The asymmetry of the plan is shown up by the chimneys rising at will. The large hip roof of iron has cowls and dormers for ventilation. Boree Cabonne is an interesting Australian house not only for its form but also for its decoration. The drawing room and billiard room retain their original papered decoration, as do many of the bedrooms. In the leadlight to the front door the painted glass depicts Sydney Harbour, and the paper frieze in the billiard room is a forest of gum trees. It represents the growing nationalism that was to mark the coming of Federation in 1901 and the traditional pastoralists' taste of the late Victorian period. The house cost £4080.

The big house at Boree Cabonne built in 1897 faces east and catches the sunrise. It stands where a house had stood since the middle years of the nineteenth century. Stone pines and a bunya pine suggest an established site.

Left *The apparently balanced design is not as it appears and the quite chaotic arrangement of chimneys gives a clue to the planning of the interior. Before the house is the old pleasure garden.*

In the back hall a fine cedar staircase leads to the upper floor. The front hall is paved with encaustic tiles, which is typical of the period.

Right *All the bedrooms on the first floor have fitted cedar wardrobes and there are marble chimneypieces. Picture rails are in each room.*

When built the house had two bathrooms upstairs and a water closet downstairs off the side verandah. This room adjoins the principal bedroom and typically there is no fitted handbasin.

Above left *The ceiling is pure white and the deep wallpaper frieze locates the brass picture rod. The curtain rod and brackets are original fittings.*

Top *The drawing room which breaks the side elevation of the house is a remarkably intact late Victorian interior. There is a white Carrara marble chimneypiece, the original wallpapers and much of the original furniture and pictures.*

Left *The dining room retains some of its original furniture as well as steel engravings in oak frames. Typical of this period, all the doors have fanlights. The door on the left leads directly into the pantry.*

In the central west of Queensland the idea of the verandah reached its ultimate, with the verandah being bigger than the house itself. The verandahed bungalow at **Bimbah**, on the Thomson River, was built in 1898 by the pastoralist Edward Edkins on land he had taken up in 1890. The Edkins were a pioneering north Queensland family, Edkins' father having settled his family in the Gulf country in the 1860s. Although he had been sent south to be educated, Edkins had spent all his adult life in the north and was acquainted with the climate and the privations his family had suffered.

Like all large stations there is virtually a village at Bimbah, and one enters a large area surrounded by outbuildings. The house is to the right and sits encircled by a park rail fence and is reached across a gravelled forecourt planted with pepper trees.

Although essentially practical, it nonetheless respects architectural niceties and in effect has both an entrance front and a garden front, the kitchen and offices being at the side to the left. The house is a single pile of rooms 5.5 metres (18 feet) across with a hipped roof broken by two ventilating cowls. French doors lead into the skillion-roofed verandah 5.5 metres wide, which encircles what is basically three rooms (sitting room and two bedrooms). The real living room is the verandah, which in area is more than double the size of the house. The only external elaboration is the verandah supported by columns with moulded capitals and cast-iron brackets. Between the columns are balustrades of the simplest chinoiserie form.

The house has its studs exposed externally and is lined on the inner face with horizontal chamfer boarding. The internal cross walls are of vertical boards stiffened with intermediate cross rails like those we saw at Wyaralong.

The verandah forms the main living area of the house and is finished with an elegant balustrade and column detail. Between the columns hang chain venetians to control the sun and the air.

Top The garden front of Bimbah. The house is a single pile of rooms completely encircled by an extremely deep verandah. To the right is the separate kitchen pavilion and between the dining room formed within the verandah in the 1920s.

Left The entrance front which faces a courtyard planted with pepper trees.

Over The homestead complex seen from the approach road. In the centre is the nursery wing and to the right the main house.

Pivot-hung fanlights are above each set of french doors. The glass is covered with Glacier window decoration.

The ceilings are in a tent form. Except in the sitting room all the internal hoop-pine boarding is left unpainted and is varnished.

The external colours of oxblood and white, with an eau-de-Nil verandah ceiling and Brunswick green chain venetians to the verandah edge, exemplify the north Queensland house at the end of the century. To the right of the forecourt, in 1904, a pyramidal-roofed pavilion was built as a nursery, and this was joined to the main verandah by its own encircling verandah, which has an added awning of corrugated iron cantilevered by brackets from its columns.

Bimbah is perhaps the ultimate Australian house in the country. Australian architecture was just one hundred years old, and it had produced a house type that was recognisably Australian and our own. In essence, this has not been improved upon. The archetypal Australian country house is still equated with houses like Bimbah.

Typical of this region, the walls of Bimbah are lined only on the inside with horizontal chamfer boards and the french doors open out.

The depth of the verandah can be appreciated here. Bimbah is more verandah than house. This provides the main living area and can also be used for sleeping.

The bore water tank is the homestead's life blood. To the left is the homestead, its kitchens and domestic offices in the foreground.

The verandah of the nursery wing at Bimbah is not as deep as that of the main house.

Above left *On the right is the nursery pavilion added in 1904. As well as the encircling verandah which picks up the character of the main house it has an awning of corrugated ripple iron bracketed from its columns.*

Left *The inner face of the chamfer boards are V jointed and the boarding is carried up to create a tent form ceiling. The french doors and skirting board are of cedar. The screen at the end is a 1920s alteration in silky oak formed when the side verandah was enclosed to make a dining room. The room retains its body and border carpet and turn of the century furnishings.*

Left *In contrast to the principal living room the hoop pine boards lining the bedroom have been varnished. The partition wall shows its framing. The doorway behind the bed leads to the sitting room.*

Select Bibliography

Architectural Magazine, vols 1–5, ed. J. C. Loudon, 1836.

Australian Dictionary of Biography, vols 1–10, Melbourne University Press, Melbourne, from 1966.

BEAMES, R. O. AND WHITEHILL, J. A. E. *Some Historic Gardens of South Australia*, National Trust of South Australia, Adelaide, 1981.

BEIERS, GEORGE. *Houses of Australia*, Ure Smith, Sydney, 1948.

BELL, PETER. *Timber and Tin*, University of Queensland Press, St Lucia, Qld, 1984.

BROADBENT, JAMES, EVANS, IAN AND LUCAS, CLIVE. *The Golden Decade of Australian Architecture*, David Ell Press, Sydney, 1978.

CAMERON, RODERICK. *My Travel's History*, Hamish Hamilton, London, 1950.

CANTLON, MAURICE. *The Homesteads of Southern New South Wales 1830–1900*, Queensberry Hill Press, Carlton, Vic., 1981.

————. *Homesteads of Victoria 1836–1900*, Georgian House, Melbourne, 1967.

COX, PHILIP AND LUCAS, CLIVE. *Australian Colonial Architecture*, Lansdowne Editions, East Melbourne, 1978.

CRAIG, MAURICE. *Classic Irish Houses of the Middle Size*, Architectural Press, London, 1976.

DE BREFFNY, BRIAN AND FFOLLIOTT, ROSEMARY. *The Houses of Ireland*, Thames & Hudson, 1975.

EASTLAKE, CHARLES L. *Hints on Household Taste*, Longmans Green & Co., London, 1872.

FORGE, SUZANNE. *Victorian Splendour*, Oxford University Press, Melbourne, 1981.

FREEMAN, PETER. *The Homestead: A Riverina Anthology*, Oxford University Press, Melbourne, 1982.

GIFFORD, E. *Designs for Elegant Cottages and Small Villas*, London, 1806.

GIROUARD, MARK. *Sweetness and Light*, Oxford University Press, Oxford, 1977.

————. *The Victorian Country House*, Oxford University Press, London, 1971.

GOODWIN, FRANCIS. *Rural Architecture*, London, 1835.

GRIFFITHS, G. NESTA. *Some Northern Homes of New South Wales*, Ure Smith, Sydney, 1954.

————. *Some Southern Homes of New South Wales*, Ure Smith, Sydney, 1952.

The Heritage of Australia, Macmillan, 1981.

HERMAN, MORTON. *The Early Australian Architects and Their Work*, Angus & Robertson, Sydney, 1954.

Historic Homesteads of Australia, vol. 1, Cassell, Melbourne, 1969.

Historic Homesteads of Australia, vol. 2, Cassell, Sydney, 1976.

The History of Queensland, Its People and Industries, vols. 1–3, Adelaide, 1919–23.

HUSSEY, CHRISTOPHER. *English Country Houses: Late Georgian 1800–1840*, Country Life, London, 1958.

KERR, JOAN AND BROADBENT, JAMES. *Gothick Taste in the Colony of New South Wales*, David Ell Press, Sydney, 1980.

KERR, ROBERT. *The Gentleman's House or, How to plan English residences from the parsonage to the palace*, John Murray, London, 1864.

LAING, D. *Hints for Dwellings*, London, 1800.

LEGOE, M. I. *A Family Affair*, Dominion Press, Maryborough, Vic., 1982.

LOUDON, J. C. *Encyclopaedia of Cottage, Farm and Villa Architecture*, London, 1833.

————. *The Suburban Gardener and Villa Companion*, London, 1838.

LUGAR, R. *The Country Gentleman's Architect*, London, 1807.

McCONNEL, KENNETH. *Planning the Australian Homestead*, Ure Smith, Sydney, 1947.

PAPWORTH, J. B. *Rural Residences*, London, 1818.

The Pastoral Homes of Australia (New South Wales), Pastoralists' Review, 1910.

The Pastoral Homes of Australia (New South Wales and Queensland), Pastoralists' Review, 1911.

The Pastoral Homes of Australia (New South Wales, Queensland, South Australia and New Zealand), Pastoralists' Review, 1914.

PLAW, JOHN. *Ferme Ornée*, London, 1805.

————. *Rural Architecture*, London, 1802.

POCOCK, WILLIAM. *Architecture Designs for Rustic Cottages*, London, 1807.

Priceless Heritage, Platypus Publications, Hobart, 1964.

RICHARDSON, C. J. *The Englishman's House from a Cottage to a Mansion*, London, 1870.

ROBERTSON, E. GRAEME. *Adelaide Lace*, Rigby, Adelaide, 1973.

————. *The Early Buildings of Southern Tasmania*, Georgian House, Melbourne, 1970.

ROBERTSON, E. GRAEME AND CRAIG, EDITH N. *The Early Houses of Northern Tasmania*, vols 1 and 2, Georgian House, Melbourne, 1964.

SAUNDERS, DAVID (ed.). *Historic Buildings of Victoria*, Jacaranda Press, Brisbane, 1966.

SOANE, JOHN. *Sketches in Architecture*, London, 1798.

STEVENSON, J. J. *House Architecture*, London, 1880.

TANNER, HOWARD (ed.). *Architects of Australia*, Macmillan, Melbourne, 1981.

TARBUCK, E. L. *The Builder's Practical Director*, Leipzig and Dresden, 1855.

TAYLOR, PETER. *An Australian Country Life*, Allen & Unwin, Sydney, 1986.

VAUX, CALVERT. *Villas and Cottages*, New York, 1857.

Victoria's Representative Men at Home, Melbourne, 1904.

WATTS, PETER. *Historic Gardens of Victoria*, Oxford University Press, Melbourne, 1983.

WICKES, C. *A Handy Book of Villa Architecture*, London, 1859.

Glossary

acroterion Formalised ornamental upstand, placed on the extremities of a gable apex in classical architecture. Appears in Australia as a galvanised iron cutout placed at the corners of gutters.

adobé Unburnt brick, dried in the sun.

adze Tool with a very sharp blade at right-angles to the handle and curving in towards it, used for the smoothing or shaping of rough timber.

apse Semi-circular or polygonal recess termination of a church sanctuary; first applied to a Roman basilica.

apsidal Curved end of a building, either semi-circular or elliptical.

arcade Series of arches supported on piers or columns. *See also* loggia.

arcading Rows of small arches (often blind) forming arcades, but used solely for decoration.

arch Structure forming the head of an opening and in which all the materials are in compression; usually curved (partly circular or elliptical), but sometimes flat. *See also* blind arch; ogee-headed arch; segmental arch.

architraves Name for the collective parts that surround a doorway or window; the ornamental moulding around the exterior of an arch.

art nouveau Period of art that succeeded Victorian eclecticism; superficially based upon the tendrils of plants and other sinuous forms.

ashlar (work) Term applied to carefully wrought building stones.

atrium (plan) In Roman architecture, the outer or entrance court, surrounded by a roof, but open to the sky in the centre.

attic storey In classical architecture, an upper storey placed above the level of the main cornice.

awning Roof with an open side, supported by posts, brackets or cantilevering.

axial Any form rotating from an axis or axes.

balcony Balustraded platform with access from an upper floor level.

baluster Post between the newel posts of a staircase that helps to support the handrail; a pear- or urn-shaped pillar, usually of stone, supporting a railing.

balustrade Series of balusters supporting a handrail or coping.

base Foundation or bottom; base course; the lower portion of any architectural feature.

batten Small timber member spanning between central supports, usually for the support of shingles, tiles or linings.

bay Recess; projecting window space, circular or geometric in shape.

bay window Angular or curved projection of a house-front containing fenestration. If curved, also called bow window; if on an upper storey only, known as an *oriel* or *oriel window*. *See also* bow window.

bead Small cylindrical moulding, often carved with an ornament resembling a string of beads.

beam Long piece of squared timber spanning between supports.

bearers Small and subsidiary wooden joists used to support the boarding of a lead gutter; the winders of a staircase. The term now usually applies to the heavier timbers that rest on the stumps of piers to take the floor joists.

blind arch Arch without an opening.

boarding Erection of boards or combination of thin timber sheets to form a cover.

bolection Moulding used to cover the joint between two members with different surface levels; projects beyond both surfaces.

bollard Cast-iron or stone post on roadway to protect a kerb, wall, etc., or to indicate a traffic diversion.

bond Method of overlapping bricks or stone to bind them together in a wall. There are a number of usual methods that are recognisable from the pattern of header and stretcher bricks on the wall face, e.g. English bonding, Flemish bonding, colonial bonding, with stretcher bonding being the most common in present-day work.

bow window Curved bay window in a regular circular or eliptical form. *See also* bay window.

bracing Piece of timber to strengthen or make firm a timber frame; a diagonal piece checked into the studs and plates of an open wall frame.

bracket Small supporting piece of stone, wood, etc., to carry a projecting horizontal member.

breakfront Broken facade of a building created by the insertion of a pediment or other architectural device.

breast panel Panelled frame between a windowsill and the floor.

breezeway Open passageway created within a building for the purpose of ventilation.

bressummer Beam extending horizontally over a large opening and sustaining a wall, awning, etc., especially above shop windows.

brick-nogging Timber partition with bricks between the studs.

broach spire Octagonal spire rising without a parapet above a tower, with pyramidal forms at the angles of the tower.

bungalow Literally, a Bengal house; a single-storey house with large overhanging roofs, supported by posts or piers.

butt To place two architectural objects together so that they touch.

buttress Mass of masonry or brickwork built against a wall to provide stability or to counteract the outward thrust of an arch or vault behind it.

caisson Watertight chamber used in laying foundations under water.

canopy Roof-like covering with small supports.

cantilever Structural member that projects beyond the line of support; being held down by the superincumbent weight of a wall, or in some other way, it is capable of bearing the weight along the line of projection.

capital In classical architecture, the uppermost part of a column or pilaster, situated between the shaft and the entablature.

caryatid porch Porch supported by sculptured female figures; traditionally taken to represent women of Caria who sided with the Persians against the Greeks and were made slaves.

casement Window hinged on one of its edges, opening inwards or outwards.

caulicoli Small volutes under the flowers on the abacus to the Corinthian capital.

ceiling Under-surface of the top of a room.

chair rail Rail surrounding a room at approximately one metre from floor, to prevent damage to plaster surface.

chinoiserie European imitations of evocations of Chinese art.

Church Commissioners' Gothic Examples of Gothic architecture produced on a low budget and resulting from the dictates of the English Church Commissioners; usually picturesque Gothic.

clerestory Upper stage in a building, with windows above adjacent roofs.

clinkers Bricks from the hottest part of the kiln that have been over-burnt and vitrified. They are usually extremely hard, dark in colour and often, having fused together in the firing, have to be broken apart, leaving jagged surfaces.

cobblestones Water-worn rounded stones used for paving.

coffer Sunken panel, caisson or lacunaria formed in ceilings, vaults and domes.

colonial architecture (Australian) Period of architecture between 1788 and 1850 in Australia.

colonial revival Architecture produced post-1900 in the manner and style of Australian colonial architecture.

coping Capping course at the top of a brick or stone wall, a balustrade or similar.

corbel Block of stone projecting from a wall, supporting some structure.

Corinthian One of the orders of classical architecture; distinguished by its bell-shaped capital, ornamented with acanthus, olive, or laurel leaves, from which eight small volutes or caulicoli emerge. The shaft is normally fluted.

cornice In classical architecture, the top section of the entablature. Also a projecting decorative feature along the top of a wall, arch, etc.

corona Wide, overhanging flat member to an outside cornice, with throating or drip to throw the water from the face of the wall.

cortile Italian name for an internal court, surrounded by an arcade.

cottage ornée Artfully rustic building, usually of asymmetrical plan.

course Layer of bricks, stone, etc. in building.

cusp Point formed by the intersection of the foils in Gothic tracery.

dado Lower part of an internal wall, especially when faced or coloured differently from the upper part.

dentils In classical architecture, small rectangular blocks placed in rows, like teeth, usually set in the cornice of a building.

detailing Expression of a particular shape or form to describe minutely or circumstantially.

diaper All-over pattern of carved or painted elements, usually of small square or lozenge shapes.

Doric One of the orders of classical architecture; primarily distinguished by the triglyphs and metopes in its frieze and the mutules under its corona. The Greek Doric column has a fluted shaft, but no base, whereas the Roman column has a base and a fluted or unfluted shaft.

dormer (window) Window placed vertically in the sloping plane of a roof.

double-pile plan Plan that has four rooms on each floor or two rooms in depth.

dowel Small piece of timber, square or circular, inserted into a joint, usually in masonry or timber, to hold two pieces together.

dower house A secondary house on a country property, usually for a widow on her deceased husband's estate.

drafted margin Dressed edge of stone, usually carved smooth.

dressing (of stone) Smoothing and finishing of stone, as when it is to be used in the elevational treatment of walls, at the angles (i.e. quoins) of a building, or in frames for doors and windows.

dripstone Projection of stone that sheds the water away from the wall of a building. In windows, singular or continuous to walls.

eaves Projecting edge of a roof that overhangs the walls.

eclectic (architecture) Borrowed or copied architecture.

egg-and-dart Ornament of alternating egg-like and sharp dart- or tongue-like forms.

Elizabethan (architecture) Style of architecture derived from the Elizabethan period.

end bay Bay or part of a building at the end of an architectural composition.

entablature In classical architecture, the whole of the horizontal members above a column, including architrave, frieze and cornice.

entasis Swelling or curving outwards along the outline of a column shaft, designed to counteract the optical illusion that gives a shaft, bounded by straight lines, the appearance of curving inwards.

express Pronounced, as in a work of art or architecture.

facade Face or elevation of a building.

facing Outer skin of a building, usually referred to as masonry.

fanlight Originally a window with a semi-circular head, but now applies to all windows over a door and forming part of the door opening.

fascia Flat on-edge member finishing the edge of a roof.

Federation style Period of Australian architecture between 1901 and the First World War.

fenestration Arrangement given to windows upon a wall and their associated ornament.

filigree Delicate open-work design.

finial Top of a canopy, gable or pinnacle.

french window Long window opening serving for exit and entrance.

fret, fretted (work) Interlaced open work of wood, stone or metal.

frieze Middle division of a classical entablature; often decorated.

gable Triangular portion of a wall, between the enclosing lines of a sloping roof; in classical architecture, this formed a pediment.

gallery Covered walk, raised floor or balcony over part of the area of a church.

galvanise Strictly, to coat a metal by electrical-chemical action. When used as 'galvanised iron', to coat iron with zinc, usually by dipping or spraying rather than by galvanic action.

Georgian Style term loosely used for English eighteenth-century architecture, together with decoration, furniture and silver produced at any time during the reign of the first three Hanovarian kings (1714–1820); also their derivatives in the United States, Australia and elsewhere.

glazing bar Wood or metal bar within the window-sash that holds the glass.

Gothic In the pointed arch style of medieval architecture.

Gothic label moulds A dripstone over an archway which extends across the top as well as partly down the sides of the opening.

Gothic revival Revival of the Gothic style that imitated the pointed style of medieval architecture. It flourished in the later eighteenth and nineteenth centuries.

guilloche Circular interlaced ornament, like net work.

half-landing Intermediate level in a staircase between floors.

header Brick laid so that one end forms part of the face of the brickwork.

hipped (roof) Roof with sloped instead of vertical ends.

hood moulding Projecting moulding over an arch or lintel to throw off water. Also called *dripstone* or *label*.

infill Treatment of architectural surfaces defined between planes.

inglenook Low-ceilinged recess, with seating, about a fireplace or window.

Ionic One of the orders of classical architecture; distinguished by the volutes of its capital and the dentils in its cornice. It invariably possesses a base and is usually fluted.

Italianate (architecture) Style of architecture derived from Renaissance Italy. Embraces the architectural styles of Florence, Rome and Venice. Irregular and picturesque. Usually nineteenth century.

jalousies Blinds or shutters made with slats that slope upwards from without so as to exclude rain and sun and admit air.

jerkin-headed A gable which changes to hip at the top.

joists One of the timbers laid horizontally, or nearly so, on which the boards of a floor or the ceiling, etc. are nailed or fixed.

keystone Middle stone in an arch.

label Rectangular moulding projecting over the head of a doorway or window.

lacunaria Caissons or panels formed in ceilings, vaults and domes.

lancet (arch) Arch with an acutely pointed head.

lancet (window) Tall, narrow window with an acutely pointed head; much used in early English Gothic architecture of the thirteenth century.

lantern Small circular or polygonal structure erected on a dome or roof in order to admit light.

lattice Pattern of square or diamond laths or strips formed by placing pliant timber or other material to form a screen.

ledged and braced Applied to doors or other fitments that are constructed with a transverse piece of timber shouldered under and on top of horizontal pieces.

lintel Horizontal member that spans an opening.

loggia Open-sided arcade.

louvre Overlapping slips of timber, glass or other thin material, arranged with spaces between to exclude rain but to admit air.

lyncrusta Heavily embossed wallpaper.

mansard roof Roof with two contiguous slopes, the lower being steeper than the upper; named after the French architect François Mansard (1598–1666).

metopes (Greek: *meta* = between, *ope* = opening). The space between Doric triglyphs, sometimes left open in ancient examples.

moulding Projecting or recessed bands used to ornament a wall or other surface; may be plain or enriched. Each style of architecture produces its characteristic mouldings. *See also* architraves; dripstone; egg-and-dart; hood moulding; label; run mould; scotia.

mouth To check out a triangular piece of a rafter where it contacts the top plate.

mullion Vertical stay dividing a window into lights.

mutules Projecting inclined blocks in Doric cornices; supposed to be derived from the ends of wooden rafters.

neo-classicism Period of architecture that copied Greek and Roman architecture in the seventeenth, eighteenth and nineteenth centuries.

newel, newel post Central pillar from which the steps of a winding stair radiate. Also the principal posts at the angles and end of a square staircase, supporting the outer string and hand-rail.

nogging In timber structures, those pieces of timber built between studs, rafters, joists, etc., either to strengthen the structure or to fix linings etc.

ogee-headed arch Pointed arch formed of two convex arcs above and two concave arcs below; used particularly in late Gothic and Muslim architecture.

ogee canopies (cusps and quatrefoils) Moulding made up of a convex and a concave curve.

order Architectural style and the proportions between the parts of a complete column and its entablature. The classical orders are either Greek (Doric, Ionic, Corinthian) or Roman (Tuscan, Doric, Ionic, Corinthian, Composite).

oriel Bay window projecting from an upper storey, usually supported on corbels.

ormolu Applied furniture ornaments of gold-coloured alloy of copper, zinc and tin, gilded bronze or lacquered brass.

palisade Fence of pointed wooden or metal stakes.

Palladian Pertaining to the works of the Italian architect, Andrea Palladio (1508–80).

palazzo Italian palace.

panel Distinct part of a surface, especially a door or wall; (long) narrow rectangular board.

parapet Low wall, originally serving to protect any edge where there was a sudden drop.

paterae Flat circular ornaments that resemble the classical saucers used for wine in sacrificial libations.

pattern-book copy-book Books on architecture produced in the seventeenth, eighteenth and nineteenth centuries from which lay people could choose architectural designs.

pavilion Light, ornamental building.

pebble-dash Process of rendering buildings with small stones 'dashed' on. *See also* roughcast.

pediment In classical architecture, a triangular piece of wall above the entablature that fills in and supports the sloping roof. In Renaissance architecture, any roof-end, whether triangular, broken or segmental. *See also* gable.

pergola Open trellis-like roof intended for supporting climbing plants. *See also* treillage.

piazza Square; place derived from Italian architecture.

picked Rough texture formed by picking with a chisel.

picturesque Irregular and asymmetrical forms of beauty considered appropriate to a picture.

pier Mass of masonry, as distinct from a column, from which an arch springs in an arcade or bridge.

pilaster Flat-faced pier attached to a wall; usually designed in conformity with one of the orders of classical architecture.

pillar Slender upright structure of stone, wood, etc.; used as a support or standing alone as a monument.

pinnacle Small pointed turret crowning a buttress or roof.

pisé Rammed earth or clay.

pitch Slope of a roof measured either in degrees above the horizontal or as a ratio of the vertical rise of the roof to its span.

plaster-lined Surface spread with soft plastic mixture of lime and sand; spread on ceilings, walls, etc. and hardening to a smooth surface.

plate Horizontal timber on a wall to distribute the load from other timbers.

plinth Slightly projecting base of a column or a building.

plugging Placing of a stiff mixture of clay, vegetable fibre, cow dung and water into the interstices between untrimmed timber logs, placed between two slabs in the erection of a slab building; necessary for the weather-proofing of the building.

pointing In brickwork, the strong mortar finishing given to the exterior of the joints.

porch Covered approach to the entrance of a building.

porch in antis Recessed porch of a building.

porte-cochere Porch large enough for wheeled vehicles to pass through.

portico Porch supported by columns and open on at least one side.

portico in antis Recessed portico of a building.

puddle Clay mixed with water and sand into a semi-liquid state.

purlins Transverse horizontal timbers carrying the common rafters upon which the battens for slates, tiles, iron or any other roof covering are fastened.

quatrefoil In tracery, a panel divided by cusps into four leaf-shaped openings.

quoins Dressed stones at the angle of a building. Sometimes all the stones are of the same size; more often, they are alternately large and small.

rafter Rectangular-shaped piece of timber placed on edge that gives slope and form to a roof and on which rest the battens for the outer covering of tiles, slate or thatch, etc.

railing Level or sloping bar as part of a fence, gate, etc.

reeded To imitate a bundle of reeds by grooving either timber or masonry.

reel Turned piece of timber in the shape of a cotton-reel.

Regency Style-term properly applicable to English art and its derivatives during the time when George IV was Prince Regent (1811–20), but also used for the period of his reign (1820–30); marked by elegance and a refinement of classical forms.

Renaissance (architecture) Architecture produced in Europe in the fifteenth and sixteenth centuries.

rendered (wall) External wall to which a coat of mortar or stucco has been applied. *Render* is also the first coat of plaster on an internal wall.

reveal Side of a doorway, window or similar opening in a wall, in so far as it is revealed (i.e. not covered by the door or window frame, etc.).

ridge Line of intersection produced by two sides of a sloping or pitched roof. The piece of timber along the line of the ridge upon which rests the upper ends of the rafters is known as the *ridge board*.

riser Vertical part of a step between the treads.

Romantic (architecture) Architecture related to feeling rather than reason; architecture opposed to the classical.

roof-plane Area of roof when observed in a true plane.

roof-truss Triangular framework constructed of wood or steel for supporting the roof coverings.

rosette Small, flat, circular or oval ornament, often decorated with acanthus leaves or rose petals.

roughcast External rendering of rough material usually applied in two coats of lime, cement and sand on to which gravel etc. is thrown before the second coat is dry; also called *pebble-dash*.

roundel Round or oval-shaped medallion-like ornament.

rubble Waste fragments of stone, brick, etc.

run mould To manufacture a continuous moulding.

rustication Ashlar work of stone blocks, with only the sides wrought and the faces rough or specially rock-faced; or ashlar work of smooth-faced blocks, with the joints greatly emphasised (smooth rustication). If the horizontal joints alone are emphasised, known as *banded rustication*.

sarking Secondary protective sheeting beneath the roof or wall finish.

scotia Concave moulding.

screen Partition partly shutting off part of a room etc.; especially that between the nave and choir of a church.

scrim Cotton or linen fabric used as base for wallpaper.

segmental arch Arch of which the contour is an arc of a circle, but less than a semi-circle.

semi-basement Partially buried part of a building.

shaft Portion of a column between the base and the capital.

shingles Thin pieces of wood with parallel sides, used for roofs instead of slates, tiles, etc. Usually split but can be sawn.

single-pile plan Plan with two rooms per floor or one room deep.

skillion One-pitched roof on an addition to a house or on a detached shed or other building. Many verandahs have skillion roofs.

skirting Board placed around the bottom of the wall of a room.

slab construction Walls made by splitting lengths of tree trunk with wedges and either erecting them vertically in the ground or fitting them into grooves in wall-plates.

soffit Under horizontal face of an architrave or overhanging cornice; undersurface of a lintel or arch; a ceiling.

stucco To plaster externally with a special gypsum-lime-cement plaster, suitable for modelling and moulding.

stud Post; upright supporting timber, vertical wall members between top and bottom plates to which the wall lining, either internal or external, or both, is fixed.

stump Part of a felled or fallen tree that remains projecting from the ground; in vernacular architecture, foundations.

style Expression of fashion in the vocabulary of architecture.

swag In classical architecture, an ornamental festoon of flowers, fruit and foliage, fastened up at the sides and curving downwards in the middle. The ends of a swag often drop vertically from the fastened sides.

tenon End of a piece of wood shaped to fit into a corresponding cavity or mortice.

terrace Row of houses with adjoining side walls and built in a uniform, or almost uniform, style.

tetra-style Portico of four columns.

thatch Interwoven straw, rushes, reeds or any other vegetable substance used to cover and seal the roof and walls of a building.

tie-beam Roof-beam that spans the space from wall-plate to wall-plate.

tongue Extension of timber fashioned in the form of a tongue, which fits within another orifice, for the purpose of fixing.

tracery In Gothic architecture, an arrangement of intersecting stone-moulded bars forming patterns in the heads of pointed windows.

transom Horizontal part of a frame between the lights of a window or, in a doorway, above a door and below its fanlight.

tread Flat, horizontal part of a step.

treillage Trellis, usually in steel or timber.

triglyphs Blocks with vertical channels that form a distinguishing feature in the frieze of a Doric entablature.

truss Framed structure, usually triangulated, designed to bear a superincumbent weight; e.g. a roof-truss.

turret Small tower, usually of round or polygonal plan.

Tuscan (architecture) Architecture originating in Tuscany in Italy; expressed mostly in a simplified Doric capital.

upstand Portion of the lead of a gutter or flat turned up against a wall.

valence Descending or down-hanging drapery, usually hanging around a bed, from the head of window, etc.; or any ornamental overhanging wood or steel work.

valley Re-entrant angle formed by the intersection of two roof-planes; opposite of a hip. *See also* hip.

vault An arched masonry roof.

verandah External structure attached to a building, covered with an awning supported on one side by a wall of the building and on its outer edge by posts.

vermiculated Carved or moulded to present the appearance of worm-holes or worm-tracks.

vernacular (architecture) Constructional technique traditional to a region.

vestry Chamber associated with a church, for the purpose of robing or storage of vestments.

villa Originally an Italian farmhouse or country estate. In the eighteenth century, the word was applied to a residence in a rural or suburban situation and standing in its own grounds. It was usually occupied by a person of position or wealth. In the second half of the nineteenth century, in Australia, the term was often applied to any detached house or cottage, usually asymmetrical in plan.

volutes Scroll or spiral occurring in Ionic, Corinthian and Composite capitals.

voussoir Wedge-shaped stone used in arch construction.

wainscoting Wooden panelling to a certain height on a wall of a room.

winders Treads of steps used in a winding, curved or angled staircase; cut wider at one end than the other.

windowcase Trim or finish to a window opening to contain the sash.

window-frame Head, jamb or yoke and sill of a window.

window-sash Frame containing the glass of a window; the movable part of a window.

wreathing Curving of a hand-rail in the absence of a newel.

Index

Adams, Maurice B.   102
Allison, Francis   36
Alton   91–93
Anglo-Indian style   10, 36
Archer, Mrs Alister   64, 66
Archer, Charles   64
Archer, Colin   64
Archer, Edward   69
Archer, Joseph   14, 22
Archer, Mrs Robert   64, 66
Archer, Thomas   42, 46
Archer, William   46, 48, 69, 72, 73
Arts and Crafts movement   86, 89, 92, 109, 111

Bagot, John   97, 98
Bagot, Walter   97, 98
Baird, Thomas   59
Barr Smith, Robert   104
Barr Smith, Tom   104
Barry, Charles   18
Bayer, Ernest   97
Bicton   19–20
Bimbah   117–121
Blackburn, James   50
Blackwood   111–113
Blaxland, John   54
Bookanan   26
Boree Cabonne   114–116
Brougham, Patrick   56
Burrungurroolong   85–86
Bush Greek   29
Butler, Walter   111

Caerleon   102
Cambria   18
carpenters' Gothic style   103
Clairville   10, 36
Clarendon   22–23, 34
Clayton, Henry   20
Clayton, William   20, 21
Corney, Robert   9
Coswell   28
Cox, James   22
Crace, Edward   77
Crace, John Gregory   77
Craig, Maurice   8
Cressbrook   40–45, 60, 64, 69
Cressbrook Cottage   42

Dalness   27
D'Ebro, Charles   96
de Little, Robert   27
Dennis, Alexander   79
Dods, Robin   41, 42, 43, 77
Durham Hall   24–25, 42

E. S. & A. Bank, Melbourne   92
Eastlake, Charles   92
Edkins, Edward   117
Eeyeuk   79–81, 100
English Ecclesiological Society   70
Evans, Jack   55

Faithfull, William   66
ferme ornée   16
Forcett House   10–13
Forest Lodge   97–98
Frankfield   75–76
Franklyn Vale   76–77
Fulton, G. E.   98, 103

Gall, James   86
gardens   18, 22, 24, 25, 31, 53, 60, 61, 64, 68, 77, 79, 83, 87, 97, 98
Gardiner, Robert   86
Gatenby, Andrew   19
Gibson, Andrew   85, 86
Glasson, John   26
Gordon, James   10
Gothic style   22, 29, 33, 34, 55, 67, 70, 71, 97–98
Government House, Melbourne   86
Government House, Sydney   8, 36
Gracemere   62–66, 92
Greek revival   9, 14–15, 19, 20, 21, 29, 30
Greenup, Alfred 105

Hamilton, Alexander   79, 100
Hartwood   56–57
Hemmings of Bristol   57
Hill, George   24, 25
Hill River   55
Hopkins, Henry   31
Horn, William   102, 103, 104
Hume, Francis Rawdon   75

Irish architecture   8, 20, 21, 34
Italianate style   18, 19, 27, 34, 46, 50, 57, 66, 67, 72, 73, 79, 83, 85

Joyce, Alfred   70, 71, 83

Kean, Hugh   30
Kermode, Robert   72
Kerr, Robert   72, 85, 86
Killymoon   34–35, 82
Koch, J. A. B.   75

Lake House   9
Lamb, Edward Buckton   66, 68
Leake, Charles Henry   52
Leake, John   50
Lethaby, William   111
Longerenong   69
Loudon, J. C.   18, 38, 41, 50, 51, 66, 67, 75

Macarthur, John   59
McArthur, Peter   96
McConnel, David   41, 42
MacDonald, Campbell   100
McFarlane, Allan   105
MacKinnon, Allan,   27
Malahide   10, 16–17, 26
Manifold, Sir Chester   102
Manifold, Edward   88, 89
Manifold, James Chester   100, 102
Manifold, Thomas   88, 89, 102
Mansfield, George Allen   85
Marybank   36, 38–39
Melbourne Club   82
Meningoort   92, 94–96
Meredith, George   18
Mintaro   86–87
Mona Vale   72–73, 75, 82, 105
Morningside   30
Morris, William   86, 104, 111
Mort, Henry   76, 77
Mount Pleasant   69

Nash, John   34
neo-classicism   9, 10, 15, 22
New South Wales
    Bookanan   26
    Boree Cabonne   114–116

Burrungurroolong   85–86
Durham Hall   24–25
Frankfield   75–76
Hartwood   56–57
Perricoota   73–75
Pomeroy   33
Springfield   66–69
The Springs   59–63
Wingecarribee   57–59
Yanga   78–79
Nicholas, George   92
Nicholson, Sir Charles   78
Northbury   69–70
Norwood   70–71

O'Halloran Giles, Thomas   104
Oxley, Henry   57

palazzo style   18, 70, 82
Panshanger   14–15, 22, 29, 69
papier mâché   23, 33, 49, 57, 58, 59
pattern books   9, 10, 18, 38, 41, 85
Perricoota   73–75, 105
Philp, Colin   100
Pomeroy   33
Purchas, Albert   88, 89
Purchas, Guyon   91, 101

Queen Anne style   102–103, 111, 112
Queensland
    Bimbah   117–121
    Cressbrook   40–45
    Franklyn Vale   76–77
    Gracemere   62–66
    Wyaralong   98–100
    Wylarah   107–110

Ratho   29
Regency style   16, 19, 31, 36, 53
Reed, Joseph   82
Reid, Alexander   29
Rhodes   53–54
Richmond Hill   8, 20
Ritchie, Robert Blackwood   111
Robertson, Alexander   75, 96
Robinson, Robert   55
Rosedale   50–52, 85
Ross, William   82, 86

Scottish architecture   30
Sedding, J. D.   111
Shaw, Norman   92, 111
Shepherd, Thomas   36, 38, 72
Sinclair, John   10, 36
Smith, Lancelot   114
Soane, Sir John   14, 34
South Australia
    Forest Lodge   97–98
    Hill River   55
    Marybank   36, 38–39
    Wairoa   102–104
    Wellington Lodge   105–107
Springfield   66–69
Stewart & Harley   105, 106
Streanshalh   36, 74
Summerholme   31–33, 91

Talbot, William   16, 17
Talindert 100–102, 114
Tarbuck, E. L.   85

Tasmania
    Bicton   19–20
    Cambria   18
    Clairville   10
    Clarendon   22–23
    Coswell   28
    Dalness   27
    Forcett House   10–13
    Killymoon   34–35
    Lake House   9
    Malahide   16–17
    Mona Vale   72–73
    Morningside   30
    Northbury   69–70
    Panshanger   14–15
    Ratho   29
    Rhodes   53–54
    Richmond Hill   8
    Rosedale   50–52
    Streanshalh   36
    Summerholme   31–33
    Wickford   20–21
    Woolmers   46–49
Terry, Leonard   70, 71, 82
The Gums   82–84
The Springs   59–63, 98
Thomson, Alexander   30
Thomson, Claudius   30
Tudor revived style   70, 108, 111

Vanbrugh, Sir John   22
Vaux, Calvert   69, 72, 85, 98
verandahs in Australia   36
Verdon, Sir George   91–92
Victoria
    Alton   91–93
    Blackwood   111–113
    Eeyeuk   79–81
    Meningoort   92, 94–96
    Mintaro   86–87
    Norwood   70–71
    Talindert   100–102
    The Gums   82–84
    Wiridgil   88–91
von Stieglitz, Frederick   34

Wagner, John   75
Wairoa   102–104
Walker, Thomas   53
wallpaper   10, 31, 32, 48, 49, 51, 72, 81, 96, 98, 104, 115, 116
Wardell, William   92
Wellesley, Lord Gerald   34
Wellington Lodge   105–107
Werribee Park   79
Wickford   20–21, 101
Wingecarribee   57–59
Wiridgil   88–91, 96, 102
Woolmers   15, 46–49, 53, 98
Woore, Thomas   33
Wyaralong   98–100, 117
Wylarah   107–110

Yanga   78–79